OPPOSING
VIEWPOINTS®
SERIES

Mental Illness

Other Books of Related Interest:

Opposing Viewpoints Series

Addiction

Behavioral Disorders

Dietary Supplements

Women's Health

At Issue Series

Should Vaccinations Be Mandatory?

Teen Suicide

Alcohol Abuse

Are Americans Overmedicated?

Cancer

Do Veterans Receive Adequate Health Care?

Current Controversies Series

Drug Legalization

Poverty and Homelessness

Medicare

"Congress shall make no law . . . abridging the freedom of speech, or of the press."

First Amendment to the US Constitution

The basic foundation of our democracy is the First Amendment guarantee of freedom of expression. The Opposing Viewpoints series is dedicated to the concept of this basic freedom and the idea that it is more important to practice it than to enshrine it.

OPPOSING
VIEWPOINTS®
SERIES

Mental Illness

Noah Berlatsky, Book Editor

GREENHAVEN PRESS
A part of Gale, Cengage Learning

GALE
CENGAGE Learning·

Farmington Hills, Mich • San Francisco • New York • Waterville, Maine
Meriden, Conn • Mason, Ohio • Chicago

GALE
CENGAGE Learning

Judy Galens, *Manager, Frontlist Acquisitions*

© 2016 Greenhaven Press, a part of Gale, Cengage Learning.

Gale and Greenhaven Press are registered trademarks used herein under license.

For more information, contact:
Greenhaven Press
27500 Drake Rd.
Farmington Hills, MI 48331-3535
Or you can visit our Internet site at gale.cengage.com

For product information and technology assistance, contact us at

Gale Customer Support, 1-800-877-4253

For permission to use material from this text or product, submit all requests online at www.cengage.com/permissions

Further permissions questions can be emailed to permissionrequest@cengage.com

Articles in Greenhaven Press anthologies are often edited for length to meet page requirements. In addition, original titles of these works are changed to clearly present the main thesis and to explicitly indicate the author's opinion. Every effort is made to ensure that Greenhaven Press accurately reflects the original intent of the authors. Every effort has been made to trace the owners of copyrighted material.

Cover image © KN/Shutterstock.com.

LIBRARY OF CONGRESS CATALOGING-IN-PUBLICATION DATA

Berlatsky, Noah.
  Mental illness / Noah Berlatsky.
    pages cm. -- (Opposing viewpoints)
  Includes bibliographical references and index.
  ISBN 978-0-7377-7512-9 (hardback) -- ISBN 978-0-7377-7513-6 (paperback)
  1. People with mental disabilities--Juvenile literature. I. Title.
  HV3004.B46 2015
  616.89--dc23
                        2015023345

Printed in the United States of America
1 2 3 4 5   20 19 18 17 16

Contents

Chapter 3: Is Involuntary Treatment for the Mentally Ill Ethical?

Chapter 4: What Are Issues Surrounding Violence and the Mentally Ill?

Why Consider
Opposing Viewpoints?

> *"The only way in which a human being can make some approach to knowing the whole of a subject is by hearing what can be said about it by persons of every variety of opinion and studying all modes in which it can be looked at by every character of mind. No wise man ever acquired his wisdom in any mode but this."*
>
> *John Stuart Mill*

In our media-intensive culture it is not difficult to find differing opinions. Thousands of newspapers and magazines and dozens of radio and television talk shows resound with differing points of view. The difficulty lies in deciding which opinion to agree with and which "experts" seem the most credible. The more inundated we become with differing opinions and claims, the more essential it is to hone critical reading and thinking skills to evaluate these ideas. Opposing Viewpoints books address this problem directly by presenting stimulating debates that can be used to enhance and teach these skills. The varied opinions contained in each book examine many different aspects of a single issue. While examining these conveniently edited opposing views, readers can develop critical thinking skills such as the ability to compare and contrast authors' credibility, facts, argumentation styles, use of persuasive techniques, and other stylistic tools. In short, the Opposing Viewpoints Series is an ideal way to attain the higher-level thinking and reading skills so essential in a culture of diverse and contradictory opinions.

In addition to providing a tool for critical thinking, Opposing Viewpoints books challenge readers to question their own strongly held opinions and assumptions. Most people form their opinions on the basis of upbringing, peer pressure, and personal, cultural, or professional bias. By reading carefully balanced opposing views, readers must directly confront new ideas as well as the opinions of those with whom they disagree. This is not to argue simplistically that everyone who reads opposing views will—or should—change his or her opinion. Instead, the series enhances readers' understanding of their own views by encouraging confrontation with opposing ideas. Careful examination of others' views can lead to the readers' understanding of the logical inconsistencies in their own opinions, perspective on why they hold an opinion, and the consideration of the possibility that their opinion requires further evaluation.

Evaluating Other Opinions

To ensure that this type of examination occurs, Opposing Viewpoints books present all types of opinions. Prominent spokespeople on different sides of each issue as well as well-known professionals from many disciplines challenge the reader. An additional goal of the series is to provide a forum for other, less known, or even unpopular viewpoints. The opinion of an ordinary person who has had to make the decision to cut off life support from a terminally ill relative, for example, may be just as valuable and provide just as much insight as a medical ethicist's professional opinion. The editors have two additional purposes in including these less known views. One, the editors encourage readers to respect others' opinions—even when not enhanced by professional credibility. It is only by reading or listening to and objectively evaluating others' ideas that one can determine whether they are worthy of consideration. Two, the inclusion of such viewpoints encourages the important critical thinking skill of objectively evaluating an author's credentials and bias. This evaluation will illuminate an author's reasons for taking a particular stance on an issue and will aid in readers' evaluation of the author's ideas.

It is our hope that these books will give readers a deeper understanding of the issues debated and an appreciation of the complexity of even seemingly simple issues when good and honest people disagree. This awareness is particularly important in a democratic society such as ours in which people enter into public debate to determine the common good. Those with whom one disagrees should not be regarded as enemies but rather as people whose views deserve careful examination and may shed light on one's own.

Thomas Jefferson once said that "difference of opinion leads to inquiry, and inquiry to truth." Jefferson, a broadly educated man, argued that "if a nation expects to be ignorant and free . . . it expects what never was and never will be." As individuals and as a nation, it is imperative that we consider the opinions of others and examine them with skill and discernment. The Opposing Viewpoints series is intended to help readers achieve this goal.

David L. Bender and Bruno Leone,
Founders

Introduction

"Stigma doesn't just come from others. You may mistakenly believe that your condition is a sign of personal weakness or that you should be able to control it without help. Seeking psychological counseling, educating yourself about your condition and connecting with others with mental illness can help you gain self-esteem and overcome destructive self-judgment."

—*Mayo Clinic,*
"Mental Health: Overcoming the
Stigma of Mental Illness"

People with mental illness can face many challenges; conditions such as depression or bipolar disorder can make it difficult to work or to maintain relationships if not successfully controlled. Compounding these problems is the fear and prejudice people often feel toward those with mental illness. In fact, the Canadian Mental Health Association reports that "stigma is a reality for many people with a mental illness, and they report that how others judge them is one of their greatest barriers to a complete and satisfying life."

People with mental illness are often represented in the media as dangerous, violent, unstable, unpredictable, and irresponsible. These stereotypes can have pervasive and painful effects on mentally ill individuals. For instance, stereotypes of mental illness may be used to justify bullying or abuse, on the grounds that the mentally ill person is dangerous or brought it on themselves. A history of mental illness may also be used to deny individuals jobs or insurance, resulting in serious financial harm and making the mental illness more difficult to control or manage. "Too often and for too long, people with mental illness have been regarded by others around them as disasters waiting to happen. When we don't distinguish between people with a mental illness who are dangerous to society and those who are a danger to no one, we reinforce a pernicious idea that's both bad for society and bad for those with mental illness," said Jay Ruderman and Jo Ann Simons in an April 2015 article on the CNN website.

Because of mental health stigma, people with mental illness are often unwilling to talk about their condition for fear that they will face prejudice and discrimination. "The stigma that surrounds mental health is suffocating, and I don't feel comfortable talking about it with most of my friends and family, and certainly not my boss or colleagues," CJ Laymon wrote in the article "Why I Keep My Bipolar Disorder Secret at Work," in the *Atlantic*. Laymon has a high-stress corporate job and is afraid that revealing the disease will prevent promotions and even threaten the job itself. Managing the disease, Laymon says, is made more difficult by the inability to discuss it. "When I go to work dinners, it's awkward not to partake in the expensive bottles of wine going around—I often end up drinking at least one glass, even knowing that it could set off a hypomanic or depressive episode. The constant balancing act of managing my illness and keeping people from knowing about it creates its own stress, further compounding the issue," he explains.

At worst, the stigma of mental illness can discourage people from pursuing treatment at all. Ally Fogg writing in the *Guardian* points out, for example, that men often see mental illness as a sign of weakness. The desire to be "macho," Fogg says, prevents men from seeking help from professionals and friends, "preferring to self-medicate with alcohol or drugs with all the consequences that holds for careers, relationships, social isolation and homelessness." Fogg links the stigma men feel around mental illness to the high rates of male suicide in the United Kingdom.

A 2011 study found that in the United States, only 59.6 percent of those with a mental illness received treatment. In an essay for the Association for Psychological Science website, Patrick W. Corrigan and coauthors point out that stigma can prevent people from receiving treatment in a number of ways. Doctors who stigmatize the mentally ill may be reluctant to prescribe needed medicine or make necessary referrals because they think mentally ill individuals are malingering, or believe that they cannot really be helped. Similarly, those with mental illness can internalize the stigma and "think of themselves as unable to recover, undeserving of care, dangerous, or responsible for their illnesses." Seeing themselves as hopeless or incurable, they may not bother to seek care. Furthermore, people with mental illness may be afraid to reveal that they have the illness and may not seek out care for fear that peers or employers will find out that they are sick.

Better education can help combat stigma by teaching people that the myths they believe about mental illness are false and based on prejudice rather than facts. Legal protections, which give those with mental illness legal recourse if they are discriminated against, can also be helpful in encouraging people to seek treatment and be more open about their illnesses. In addition, when people are able to be more open about their illnesses, it can help to combat stereotypes, as coworkers and family members realize that their preconceptions about mental illness are false.

Opposing Viewpoints: Mental Illness examines issues surrounding mental disorders and illnesses in chapters titled "What Causes Mental Illness?," "How Should Mental Illness Be Treated?," "Is Involuntary Treatment for the Mentally Ill Ethical?," and "What Are Issues Surrounding Violence and the Mentally Ill?" Authors present varying viewpoints on the nature, causes, treatment, and stigma of mental illness.

OPPOSING
VIEWPOINTS®
SERIES

CHAPTER 1

What Causes Mental Illness?

Chapter Preface

Strep throat is a common bacterial infection that spreads easily through sneezing, coughing, or shaking hands. Because of its high transferability, it is one of the top ten common illnesses in children. Fortunately, it is easily treatable with antibiotics; in most cases, after a couple of days, the child is back to his or her normal activities.

In a small number of cases, however, some researchers believe strep throat may lead to a serious mental illness in children known as Pediatric Autoimmune Neuropsychiatric Disorders Associated with Streptococcal Infections, or PANDAS.

PANDAS is believed to start after a child recovers from a strep infection. The child begins to show symptoms similar to obsessive-compulsive disorder (OCD), such as excessive hand washing. There may also be unusual arm or finger motions, and in some cases more extreme symptoms, such as incontinence, fear of contact, or forgetting how to write. "We watched the child that we knew disappear in front of our eyes," the mother of a twelve-year-old diagnosed with PANDAS told a reporter in a March 2015 article for the Daily Beast.

PANDAS sounds very frightening, but doctors and researchers are not entirely sure it exists. Susan Swedo, a researcher at the National Institute of Mental Health, has had some success in proving the existence of the condition. An article by Erica Westly in *Scientific American* in January 2009 said that Swedo found, for example, that children exhibiting OCD symptoms had high levels of strep antibodies in their blood. Swedo also did experiments in which mice injected with strep antibodies engaged in abnormal, anxious behavior, which appeared to be linked to antibody deposits in the brain.

Such studies remain inconclusive, however. Dr. Nicholas Bennett, medical director of infectious diseases and immunology at Connecticut Children's Medical Center, argues that with PANDAS "it's been difficult to prove a causal link with any specific infection, or that it's an autoimmune process that is tying it all together," he said in the Daily Beast article. Other doctors worry that PANDAS is being used as an incorrect diagnosis, instead of a diagnosis of non-strep-related OCD or the neurological disorder Tourette syndrome. As a result, such patients may be given antibiotic treatments that will not help them, rather than receiving needed treatment for their conditions. Since strep is so common, it can be easy to link the onset of mental illness to a bout of the disease, some physicians worry.

Still, many doctors do think PANDAS is a real condition. Further research will make it clearer when, and whether, PANDAS causes mental illness and will provide physicians with treatments to combat it.

The authors of the viewpoints in the following chapter examine other possible causes of mental illness, including childhood trauma and chronic stress, as well as overdiagnosis of mental disorders.

> *"The fact that the medical establishment treats premenstrual symptoms as a disorder, despite lack of consensus in research, suggests that it is a sociocultural construction rather than a scientific 'fact.'"*

The Social Construction of Mental Illness: Power, Pathology and PMDD

Rachel V. Isreeli

Rachel V. Isreeli is a student at Silberman School of Social Work at Hunter College. In the following viewpoint, she argues that mental illness is a social construct rather than a biological fact. Abnormal behavior is defined by those in power, she says, who then insist that certain actions, or certain people, need medical help and readjustment. Isreeli argues that the diagnosis of premenstrual dysphoric disorder (PMDD) is an example of a socially constructed mental condition. PMDD refers to severe mood changes associated with women's menstrual cycles. Isreeli argues that women naturally experience changes with menses and that treating these changes as a medical condition contributes to sexism and inequality.

As you read, consider the following questions:

1. What is social constructivism, according to Isreeli?

2. Which natural reproductive functions does Isreeli say have been considered deviant in women?

3. According to the viewpoint, how does treatment of PMS differ in China than in Western nations?

Mental illness is a fluid construct that shifts across cultures and time periods. In Western society, mental illness is conceptualized as grounded in objective and neutral data that become enshrined in diagnostic codes such as the *Diagnostic and Statistical Manual [of Mental Disorders, DSM]*. This perception of mental illness obscures dynamics of power that shape beliefs about normality and deviance and serve to stigmatize and regulate those people who do not fit the cultural norm. Patriarchal values, which proscribe the roles and qualities of the "ideal woman," have resulted in the medicalization and pathologization of women's bodies. The case of premenstrual dysphoric disorder [PMDD] demonstrates how patriarchal values, combined with the capitalist pharmaceutical industry and the media, construct and pathologize women's regular experiences, which subsequently shapes the concept of the premenstrual body as disordered and validates pharmaceutical intervention and social control.

Social Construction, Medicalization and Pathology

Social constructionism is a conceptual framework that emphasizes the cultural and historical aspects of phenomena (Conrad & Barker, 2010). Social constructionists recognize that knowledge is not inherent, but constituted through interpersonal, institutional and social processes (Georgaca, 2013). Social constructionism highlights the social development of meaning and knowledge by examining how individuals and groups contribute to producing perceived reality (Conrad & Barker, 2010; Georgaca, 2013). Scholars in the 1960s and 1970s increasingly distanced themselves from positivist interpretations of the world that claim knowledge to be neutral and objective, asserting that social problems and deviant behavior are produced in particular contexts with intentional use of categories for social control (Conrad & Barker, 2010). This production and organization of knowledge is integral to societal power relations (Bjorklund, 2006). Foucault (1977) identifies the regulatory function of knowledge: the guise of objectivity surrounding "expert knowledge" obscures the power dynamics in the classification of categories such as "normality" and "abnormality" (Foucault, 1977; Jutel, 2011).

Social Construction of Mental Illness

The medical model of mental illness presents diagnosis as objectively based in empirical data. In contrast, Georgaca (2013) describes the constructed process: Clinical interviews are transformed into psychiatric reports through selecting only information that fits the psychiatric formulation, reformulating that information in psychiatric terms, objectifying clients through systematic deletion of their perspectives, [and] obscuring the professionals' participation . . . in order to fit the standardized sections of a psychiatric report (p. 57).

Thus, professionals have the power to privilege certain elements of a person's story while ignoring others in an effort to present a factual and "neutral" representation of a person with mental illness.

In contrast to the medical model which posits mental illness as objectively present to be discovered by scientists or physicians, social constructionists view mental illness as developed by sociocultural systems, including advocacy groups, the pharmaceutical industry, medical professionals and elected officials (Conrad & Barker, 2010; Jutel, 2011). The rise of neoliberalism and globalization has produced increasing categories and prevalence of diagnosis due to interests of commodification and consumerism (Jutel, 2011). Medicalization of regular processes is increasing, which occurs when a social situation or personal experience is made into a medical or psychological problem that requires the attention of experts (Offman & Kleinplatz, 2004).

Jutel (2011) describes diagnosis and mental illness as a sociopolitical process involving an exchange between stakeholders that ultimately produces a label to which medicine can anchor its authority. This process of labeling is embedded within competing relationships of power, control and social and financial interests (Ebeling, 2011). In a Western medical context, social power produces knowledge and the ability to name disease and disorder (Ebeling, 2011; Foucault, 1977). In his seminal book delineating the social construction of mental illness, Thomas Szasz (1961) articulates:

> Labeling people disabled by problems in living as "mentally ill" has in fact delayed recognition of the essential nature of the phenomena. At first glance, to advocate that troubled people are "sick" sounds like a great boon, for it bestows the dignity of suffering from a "real illness." But a hidden weight is attached ... which drags the troubled people back to the same sort of disability from which this semantic and social switching was to rescue them (p. 28).

The construction of illness serves to obscure underlying social problems—often due to power and oppression—and placate those who suffer by individualizing their experience and validating their issues in medical and psychological terminology.

Social Construction, Medicalization and Control of Women's Bodies

Social constructionists argue that "expert" medical knowledge reflects and reproduces existing forms of social inequality by acting as agents of social control and shoring up the interests of groups in power (Conrad & Barker, 2010; Foucault, 1988). This is accomplished through the control and elimination of problematic experiences that are defined as deviant and not adhering to social norms (Weisz & Knaapen, 2009). In patriarchal societies, women's bodies are historically pathologized in response to cultural anxieties about women's sexual and social freedoms and in effort to proscribe women's culturally "proper" role and character in society (Conrad & Barker, 2010; Offman & Kleinplatz, 2004). Foucault (1978) describes a "process whereby the feminine body was analyzed—qualified and disqualified—as being thoroughly saturated with sexuality" and integrated into medical and psychological practices (p. 104). Women's natural reproductive functions such as pregnancy, menstruation, childbirth and menopause are routinely medicalized and pathologized (Callaghan, Chacon, Coles, Botts & Laraway, 2009; Conrad & Barker, 2010; Offman & Kleinplatz, 2004). Likewise, women's emotional and psychological experiences are systematically considered deviant (Ussher, 2011). As Foucault (1988) attests, "the entire female body is riddled" by "the perpetual possibility of hysteria" (p. 153–154).

The incorporation of assumptions about women's sexuality and femininity in "objective" medicine both reflects and reproduces power relations. The process of defining deviance and sanity serves to construct and enforce boundaries of "good" behavior and unrealistic social norms for women (Andermann, 2010; Ussher, 2011).

Premenstrual Dysphoric Disorder

The case of premenstrual dysphoric disorder demonstrates the contingent and socially produced nature of mental illness and the commodification and pathologization of women's bodies and behavior.

History of PMS and PMDD

In 1931, the American gynecologist Robert Frank coined the term "premenstrual tension" (PMT) to describe a constellation of changes related to the menstrual cycle (Offman & Kleinplatz, 2004; Weisz & Knaapen, 2009). At the time, PMT provided a medical rationale for why women should stay out of the workforce and leave available jobs to men (Chrisler & Caplan, 2002). In 1953, British endocrinologist Katharina Dalton contributed to the medicalization of the menstrual cycle by introducing the term "premenstrual syndrome" (PMS) (Offman & Kleinplatz, 2004; Weisz & Knaapen, 2009). By the 1980s, PMS was firmly established in North American culture through magazines, self-help books and media (Chrisler & Caplan, 2002). It is likely no accident that the pathology of women's bodies immediately followed gains by women's liberation movements in the 1960s and 1970s. In 1987 the "disease" was institutionalized in the *DSM-III-TR* as late luteal phase dysphoric disorder (LLPDD), as an "unspecified mental disorder" presented for further study. The symptoms of LLPDD were identified as similar to PMS but more severe and debilitating. Feminist and women's groups immediately challenged LLPDD's inclusion in the *DSM*, claiming obscure, biased and inconsistent diagnostic criteria.

In 1994, the *DSM-IV* changed the name to premenstrual dysphoric disorder (PMDD), still as a category for further study (Offman & Kleinplatz, 2004). The central debate at this time focused on where PMDD should be located in the *DSM* (Offman & Kleinplatz, 2004). PMDD is now included in the main body of the *DSM-5* under "Depressive Disorders" (American Psychiatric Association [APA], 2013). The importance of PMDD's inclusion in the *DSM* cannot be understated: As the most widely known psychiatric handbook, the

DSM convinces psychotherapists and "patients" that PMDD is a mental illness (Chrisler & Caplan, 2002).

Definition and Prevalence

The *DSM-5* defines PMDD as a cluster of significantly distressing psychiatric, somatic and social symptoms such as marked affective lability (e.g., mood swings, sadness, sensitivity), irritability or anger, depressed mood, anxiety, decreased interest in activities, lethargy, change in appetite (e.g., overeating or specific food cravings) and physical symptoms (e.g., breast tenderness or swelling, "bloating" or weight gain). At least five of these symptoms must be present in the week prior to menses for at least two cycles, and must be absent during the week post-menses. Criterion D indicates that the symptoms must cause clinically significant interference with work, school, usual social activities or relationships with others. These symptoms must not be an exacerbation of another psychiatric "disorder" nor due to effects of a substance (APA, 2013).

There is a lack of consensus regarding the symptoms and prevalence of PMDD. Chrisler and Caplan (2002) have identified at least 150 changes associated with the premenstrual phase in professional and popular literature, while Halbreich et al. (2003) noted over 300 different premenstrual complaints. Offman and Kleinplatz's (2004) review of research studies indicates that anywhere between 2% to 100% of menstruating women experience symptoms associated with PMDD. The diagnostic prevalence of PMDD is inconsistent, ranging from 2–11% (Callaghan, Chacon, Coles, Botts & Laraway, 2009; Halbreich et al., 2003; Offman & Kleinplatz, 2004; Ussher, 2011).

Controversy: Culture and Constructs

In addition to lack of consensus regarding symptoms, there has been significant debate about the utility and validity of

Changing Cultural Ideas of Mental Illness

Over the past thirty years, we Americans have been industriously exporting our ideas about mental illness. Our definitions and treatments have become the international standards. Although this has often been done with the best of intentions, we've failed to foresee the full impact of these efforts. It turns out that how people in a culture think about mental illnesses—how they categorize and prioritize the symptoms, attempt to heal them, and set expectations for their course and outcome—influences the diseases themselves. In teaching the rest of the world to think like us, we have been, for better and worse, homogenizing the way the world goes mad.

There is now a remarkable body of research that suggests that mental illnesses are not, as sometimes assumed, spread evenly around the globe. They have appeared in different cultures in endlessly complex and unique forms. Indonesian men have been known to experience *amok*, in which a minor social insult launches an extended period of brooding punctuated by an episode of murderous rage. Southeastern Asian males sometimes suffer from *koro*, the debilitating certainty that their genitals are retracting into their body. Across the Fertile Crescent of the Middle East there is *zar*, a mental illness related to spirit possession that brings forth dissociative episodes of crying, laughing, shouting, and singing.

Ethan Watters, Crazy Like Us:
The Globalization of the American Psyche.
New York: Free Press, 2010.

PMDD as a diagnostic category due to unclear etiology and criteria. There have been no biological, psychological or environmental factors that explain differences between women with and without PMDD symptoms (Callaghan et al., 2009; Offman & Kleinplatz, 2004). It is possible that women with higher stress, greater incidence of sexual assault and trauma, and those who adhere to traditional feminine gender roles are at greater risk of PMDD (Chrisler & Caplan, 2002; Pérez-López, Chedraui, Pérez-Roncero, López-Baena & Cuadros-López, 2009). These correlations could suggest variables of culture, social control and marginalization, rather than pathology innate to women's psychology and biology.

Researchers have been unable to assess validity of diagnosis due to unclear operational definitions of PMDD criteria (Callaghan et al., 2009). For example, it has proven methodologically difficult to differentiate PMDD from the premenstrual exacerbation of other disorders (Criterion E) (Offman & Kleinplatz, 2004). Few studies have looked at the impact of PMDD on "usual activities" (Criterion D); rather than being operationally defined, "significant interference" is often assumed or defined arbitrarily by researchers' subjective standards (Offman & Kleinplatz, 2004).

Additional criticism concerns methodological flaws and lack of consistency in assessing, measuring and diagnosing symptoms: It is difficult to ascertain the exact phase of the menstrual cycle; there has been an absence of control groups in research; most studies are based on retrospective reports of symptoms that are influenced by cultural expectations and tend to exaggerate symptoms in Western societies (Callaghan et al., 2009; Chrisler & Caplan, 2002). Furthermore, there is controversy regarding the gendered diagnostic construct of PMDD. Callaghan et al. (2009) investigated the sex-specificity of PMDD and found that men also met provisional criteria, suggesting that the official diagnosis pathologizes women unnecessarily.

PMS and PMDD are generally considered culture-bound syndromes, which are "constellations of signs, symptoms and/or experiences that have been categorized as a dysfunction or disease in some societies but not in others" (Chrisler & Caplan, 2002, p. 284). Although notions of *symptoms* may exist worldwide, PMS and PMDD *syndromes* tend to exist in Western societies but are absent from discourse in non-Western countries (Pilver, Kasl, Desai & Levy, 2011). Ussher (2013) notes that in Eastern cultures such as Hong Kong or China, where change is accepted as a regular part of daily existence, women report physical symptoms but rarely report negative premenstrual moods.

Social Construction and Social Control

Premenstrual change is a normal female experience that is constructed as a psychological deficit. The fact that the medical establishment treats premenstrual symptoms as a disorder, despite lack of consensus in research, suggests that it is a sociocultural construction rather than a scientific "fact" (Offman & Kleinplatz, 2004). The pervasiveness of PMS and PMDD in Western culture encourages women to internalize symptoms and attribute their unhappiness, difficulties and failures to internal and biological factors rather than external stressful causes (Chrisler & Caplan, 2002). The construction of problematic premenstrual symptoms is rooted in patriarchal and capitalist values. The medicalized pathology of PMS and PMDD suggest how women *ought* to behave and thus contribute to policy and culture that authorize social control (Conrad & Barker, 2010). Western idealized femininity emphasizes women as calm, in control, slim, patient, nurturing and kind (Chrisler & Caplan, 2002; Ussher, 2011). Capitalist American culture encourages people to maintain control over their lives and ensure productivity. Since the medicalization of PMDD institutionalizes "mood swings," "irritability or anger," "weight gain," "lethargy" and "out of control" as problematic, it reinforces traditional ideals of femininity and capitalist goals while repressing legitimate and normal feelings (APA, 2013; Weisz & Knaapen, 2009).

Pharmaceutical Industry and the Media

The conceptualization of women's premenstrual changes and emotional variability as inappropriate results in workplace policy, the pharmaceutical industry and the media reinforcing practices of women's self-surveillance in regard to moods, behaviors and expressions (Chrisler & Caplan, 2002; Ussher, 2011). The pharmaceutical industry has become a major stakeholder in the process of diagnosing and publicizing PMDD, as it has recognized the profitability of constructing, commercializing and disseminating "knowledge" about premenstrual symptoms (Conrad & Barker, 2010; Ebeling, 2011; Offman & Kleinplatz, 2004).

The pharmaceutical industry supports research regarding the symptoms, prevalence, etiology and treatment of PMDD; one article for this paper was written by doctors that receive funds from Eli Lilly and Bayer Healthcare Pharmaceuticals, two companies that make prescription drugs for PMDD (Cunningham, Yonkers, O'Brien & Eriksson, 2009). In constructing and branding the "disease," Eli Lilly repackaged its top-selling antidepressant Prozac—just before the patent was due to expire—in pink and purple colors and renamed it Sarafem as a treatment for PMDD (Chrisler & Caplan, 2002; Ebeling, 2011). The industry then invests in media coverage about the "condition" for which it has a treatment: images of premenstrual problems are ubiquitous in magazines, films, television shows, songs and advertising (Chrisler & Caplan, 2002).

Together, media and the pharmaceutical industry brand the diagnosis and promote "disorder" awareness through direct-to-consumer marketing campaigns (Ebeling, 2011). These campaigns encourage self-diagnosis, as the vast majority of U.S. women of reproductive age become convinced that they suffer from PMS at least occasionally (Chrisler & Caplan, 2002; Ebeling, 2011). Bayer's website for Yaz, a birth control pill that is marketed for treatment of PMDD, provides a checklist tool for this purpose (Ebeling, 2011). With patient self-diagnosis, psychiatrists and pharmaceutical companies have an economic incentive to emphasize a psychiatric diagnosis that legitimizes the profession and validates pharmaceutical treatments (Offman & Kleinplatz, 2004).

Conclusion

Premenstrual change is a normal part of women's experience. However, Western culture constructs the premenstrual phase as a time of psychological disturbance, precisely because some of the symptoms—frustration, anger, erratic behavior, lack of "productivity"—defy norms about how women ought to behave (Conrad & Barker, 2010; Ussher, 2013). This sociomedical pathology identifies menstruation as a disorder in need of treatment, which justifies the use of psychiatric intervention that reinforces gender inequality and becomes a boon to the pharmaceutical industry with the help of the media (Conrad & Barker, 2010; Ussher, 2013). The construction of premenstrual change as a disorder serves to restrict women's behavior and ensure self-policing (Foucault, 1977): Only in a capitalist and patriarchal context does it make sense to label normal female biological processes as a disease that requires controlling. It is critical that practitioners and "patients" alike denaturalize psychiatric "knowledge" and explore the institutions and interests involved in creating and labeling pathologies.

References

American Psychiatric Association (2013). *Desk Reference to the Diagnostic Criteria from DSM-5*. Arlington, VA: American Psychiatric Association.

Andermann, L. (2010). Culture and the social construction of gender: Mapping the Intersection with mental health. *International Review of Psychiatry*, 22(5), 501–512.

Bjorklund, P. (2006). No man's land: Gender bias and social constructivism in the diagnosis of borderline personality disorder. *Issues in Mental Health Nursing* 27(3), p. 3–23.

Callaghan, G. M., Chacon, C., Coles, C., Botts, J., & Laraway, S. (2009). An empirical evaluation of the diagnostic criteria for Premenstrual Dysphoric Disorder: Problems with sex specificity and validity. *Women & Therapy*, 32(1), 1–21.

Chrisler, J. C., & Caplan, P. (2002). The strange case of Dr. Jekyll and Ms. Hyde: How PMS became a cultural phenomenon and a psychiatric disorder. *Annual Review of Sex Research*, 13, 274.

Conrad, P., & Barker, K. K. (2010). The social construction of madness: Key insights and policy implications. *Journal of Health and Social Behavior*, 51(S), S67–S79.

Cunningham, J., Yonkers, K. A., O'Brien, S., & Eriksson, E. (2009). Update on research and treatment of Premenstrual Dysphoric Disorder. *Harvard Review of Psychiatry*, 17(2), 120–137.

Ebeling, M. (2011). 'Get with the program!': Pharmaceutical marketing, symptom checklists and self-diagnosis. *Social Science & Medicine*, 73(6), 825–832.

Foucault, M. (1977). *Discipline & punish: The birth of the prison.* New York, NY: Random House.

Foucault, M. (1988). *Madness and civilization: A History of insanity in the age of reason.* New York, NY: Random House.

Foucault, M. (1978). *The History of sexuality. Volume 1: An introduction.* London: Penguin.

Halbreich, U., Borenstein, J., Pearlstein, T., & Kahn, L. S. (2003). The prevalence, impairment, impact, and burden of

Premenstrual Dysphoric Disorder (PMS/PMDD). *Psychoneuroendocrinology, 28,* Supplement 3(0), 1–23.

Georgaca, E. (2013). Social constructionist contributions to critiques of psychiatric diagnosis and classification. *Feminism & Psychology* 23(1), 56–62.

Jutel, A., & Nettleton, S. (2011). Towards a sociology of diagnosis: Reflections and opportunities. *Social Science & Medicine,* 73(6), 793–800.

Offman, A., & Kleinplatz, P. J. (2004). Does PMDD belong in the DSM? Challenging the medicalization of women's bodies. *Canadian Journal of Human Sexuality,* 13(1), 17–27.

Pérez-López, F. R., Chedraui, P., Pérez-Roncero, G., López-Baena, M. T., & Cuadros-López, J. L. (2009). Premenstrual Syndrome and Premenstrual Dysphoric Disorder: Symptoms and cluster influences. *The Open Psychiatry Journal,* 3, 39–49.

Pilver, C. E., Kasl, S., Desai, R., & Levy, B. R. (2011). Exposure to American culture is associated with Premenstrual Dysphoric Disorder among ethnic minority women. *Journal of Affective Disorders,* 130(1–2), 334–341.

Szasz, T. (1961). *The myth of mental illness: Foundations of a theory of personal conduct.* New York, NY: Hoeber-Harper.

Ussher, J. M. (2011). *The madness of women: Myth and experience.* New York, NY: Routledge.

Ussher, J. M. (2013). Diagnosing difficult women and pathologising femininity: Gender bias in psychiatric nosology. *Feminism & Psychology* 23(1), 63–69.

Ussher, J. M., & Perz, J. (2010). Disruption of the silenced self: The case of Premenstrual Syndrome. In D. C. Jack, & A. Ali (Eds.), (pp. 435–458). New York, NY: Oxford University Press.

Weisz, G., & Knaapen, L. (2009). Diagnosing and treating Premenstrual Syndrome in five Western nations. *Social Science & Medicine*, 68(8), 1498–1505.

"Children experiencing four types of trauma were 30 times more likely to have behavior and learning problems than those not exposed to trauma."

Childhood Trauma Can Lead to Mental Illness

Victor Carrion

Victor Carrion is associate professor of psychiatry and behavioral sciences at Stanford School of Medicine. In the following viewpoint, he discusses research that indicates that symptoms of mental illness, including obesity, are often the result of childhood trauma. These findings are important because pediatricians often do not look for trauma as a cause of mental illness in children. This frequently results in poor or incorrect treatment. Carrion concludes that physicians should inquire about trauma more often in their interaction with pediatric patients.

As you read, consider the following questions:

1. According to Carrion, what disorder do physicians often diagnose instead of post-traumatic stress disorder?

2. According to the viewpoint, what records did the researchers look at during their study?

3. According to Carrion, what is the Center for Youth Wellness, and what are its goals?

New research has shown that children's risk for learning and behavior problems and obesity rises in correlation to their level of trauma exposure, says the psychiatrist at the Stanford University School of Medicine and Lucile Packard Children's Hospital who oversaw the study. The findings could encourage physicians to consider diagnosing post-traumatic stress disorder [PTSD] rather than attention-deficit/ hyperactivity disorder [ADHD], which has similar symptoms to PTSD but very different treatment.

The study examined children living in a violent, low-income neighborhood and documented an unexpectedly strong link between abuse, trauma and neglect and the children's mental and physical health. It reported, for instance, that children experiencing four types of trauma were 30 times more likely to have behavior and learning problems than those not exposed to trauma.

Children Do Not Get Used to Violence

"In communities where there is violence, where children are exposed to events such as shootings in their neighborhoods, kids experience a constant environmental threat," said senior author Victor Carrion, MD, associate professor of psychiatry and behavioral sciences at Stanford. "Contrary to some people's belief, these children don't get used to trauma. These events remain stressful and impact children's physiology."

The new study is being published online today in *Child Abuse & Neglect: The International Journal*. Carrion collaborated on the research with scientists at the University of New Orleans and the Bayview Child Health Center, part of San Francisco's California Pacific Medical Center.

The findings provide compelling evidence that pediatricians should routinely screen children for trauma exposures, said Carrion, who is also a child psychiatrist at Packard Children's.

"As simple as it may seem, physicians do not ask about trauma," he said. "And kids get the wrong diagnoses."

The study builds on earlier work that linked worsening health in adults with their dose of exposure to nine types of adverse childhood events, including being subject to various kinds of abuse or neglect; having a household member who abused alcohol or drugs, was incarcerated or was mentally ill; having a mother who was treated violently; and not living in a two-parent household. Middle-class men exposed to more of these events had more chronic diseases in adulthood, the prior research found. The results of the current study highlight the need for early identification of such adversity-associated health problems and early intervention. Obesity, for example, may act as a mediator to other health problems such as diabetes, cardiac risk and inflammatory illness.

To perform the study, the researchers evaluated medical records from 701 children treated at a primary care clinic in Bayview-Hunters Point, a San Francisco neighborhood with high rates of poverty and violence. About half the children were African American; the rest came from other ethnic backgrounds. Each child's exposure to adverse events was scored on a scale from 0 to 9, with one point given for each type of adversity. The researchers also evaluated the medical records for evidence of obesity and learning or behavior problems.

Be Aware of Possible Trauma

Two-thirds of the children in the study had experienced at least one category of adversity, and 12 percent experienced four or more categories. An adversity score of 4 or higher left kids 30 times as likely to show learning and behavior problems and twice as likely to be obese as those with a score of 0.

Childhood Trauma and Health

When I met [Monisha] Sullivan, last September [2010], she had recently turned eighteen, and three days earlier she had been emancipated from foster care. She was now living alone, in a subsidized apartment off Fillmore Street. In California, emancipated foster children are given a summary of their case file, which meant that Sullivan had just been handed an official history of her rootless adolescence. "It brought up a lot of emotions," she told me. "I read it, and I kind of wanted to cry. But I was just, like, 'It's over with.'" The most painful memory was of the day, in fifth grade, when she was pulled out of class by a social worker she had never met and driven to a strange new home. It was months before she was able to have contact with her father. "I still have dreams about it," she told me. "I feel like I'm going to be damaged forever."

I asked Sullivan to explain what that damage felt like. For a teenager, Sullivan is unusually articulate about her emotional state—when she feels sad or depressed, she writes poems—and she evoked her symptoms with precision. She had insomnia and nightmares, she said, and at times her body inexplicably ached. Her hands sometimes shook uncontrollably. Her hair had recently started falling out, and she was wearing a pale-green head scarf to cover up a thin patch. More than anything, she felt anxious: about school, her daughter, even earthquakes. "I think about the weirdest things," she said. "I think about the world ending. If a plane flies over me, I think they're going to drop a bomb. I think about my dad dying. If I lose him, I don't know what I'm going to do."

Paul Tough, "The Poverty Clinic,"
New Yorker, *March 21, 2011.*

Children with an adversity score of 1 were 10 times as likely to have learning and behavior problems as those not exposed to trauma.

Prior research has shown that about 30 percent of children in violent communities have symptoms of post-traumatic stress disorder, which can include the learning and behavior problems detected in the current study, Carrion noted. However, a physician unaware of the fact that a child experienced trauma, and noting the child's physiological hyper-arousability and cognitive difficulties, may diagnose ADHD instead of PTSD. That's a problem because the two disorders have opposite treatments, he said. Kids with PTSD need psychotherapy, not the stimulant medications given for ADHD.

"Children can recover from PTSD with the appropriate treatment, which is one of approach and not avoidance," Carrion said. "By not asking about trauma, we're utilizing avoidance. We're perpetuating PTSD."

As part of their efforts to address the long-term health problems that stem from childhood trauma, Carrion, his collaborators and several San Francisco community partners are working to launch the Center for Youth Wellness, a one-stop health and wellness center for urban children and families in San Francisco. The Center for Youth Wellness will combine pediatrics with mental health services, educational support, family support, research and best practices in child-abuse response under one roof. With both public and private support, the center will coordinate the services of multiple agencies to give children a safe and accessible place to increase their resilience to adverse life experiences and improve their well-being.

The center . . . is a partnership between California Pacific Medical Center's Bayview Child Health Center, San Francisco Child Abuse Prevention Center, San Francisco district attorney's office, Stanford's Early Life Stress [and Pediatric Anxiety] Research Program at Lucile Packard Children's Hospital and Tipping Point Community. Nadine Burke, MD, director of the Bayview center, is also a coauthor of the study.

"We need to create trauma-informed systems," Carrion concluded, adding that the Center for Youth Wellness hopes to function as a model for such systems across the nation. People working for the welfare of children need to be on the lookout for trauma and know how to intervene, and how to work with the family and with schools, he said. "If trauma goes untreated, it's very costly for the individuals involved and for society in general."

> *"Chronic stress generates more myelin-producing cells and fewer neurons than normal . . . which disrupts the delicate balance and timing of communication within the brain."*

Chronic Stress Can Lead to Mental Illness

Robert Sanders

Robert Sanders is a media relations professional at the University of California, Berkeley. In the following viewpoint, he discusses research by Daniela Kaufer, an integrative biologist. Kaufer examined how stress affects the brain, and she determined that stress can impact neural connections and brain structure over time. This can make those who suffer from long-term stress more susceptible to mental illnesses, such as depression and post-traumatic stress disorder. Sanders concludes that a better understanding of brain changes can lead to better treatments for mental illnesses.

As you read, consider the following questions:

1. According to the viewpoint, what role does the hippocampus play in the brain?

2. What might result if stress creates more connections between the hippocampus and amygdala, according to Daniela Kaufer?

3. According to the viewpoint, what are synapses?

University of California [UC], Berkeley, researchers have shown that chronic stress generates long-term changes in the brain that may explain why people suffering chronic stress are prone to mental problems such as anxiety and mood disorders later in life.

Their findings could lead to new therapies to reduce the risk of developing mental illness after stressful events.

Stress Changes the Brain

Doctors know that people with stress-related illnesses, such as post-traumatic stress disorder (PTSD), have abnormalities in the brain, including differences in the amount of gray matter versus white matter. Gray matter consists mostly of cells—neurons, which store and process information, and support cells called glia—while white matter is comprised of axons, which create a network of fibers that interconnect neurons. White matter gets its name from the white, fatty myelin sheath that surrounds the axons and speeds the flow of electrical signals from cell to cell.

How chronic stress creates these long-lasting changes in brain structure is a mystery that researchers are only now beginning to unravel.

In a series of experiments, Daniela Kaufer, UC Berkeley associate professor of integrative biology, and her colleagues, including graduate students Sundari Chetty and Aaron Friedman, discovered that chronic stress generates more myelin-producing cells and fewer neurons than normal. This results in an excess of myelin—and thus, white matter—in some areas of the brain, which disrupts the delicate balance and timing of communication within the brain.

"We studied only one part of the brain, the hippocampus, but our findings could provide insight into how white matter is changing in conditions such as schizophrenia, autism, depression, suicide, ADHD [attention-deficit/hyperactivity disorder] and PTSD," she said.

The hippocampus regulates memory and emotions, and plays a role in various emotional disorders.

Kaufer and her colleagues published their findings in the Feb. 11 [2014] issue of the journal *Molecular Psychiatry.*

Does Stress Affect Brain Connectivity?

Kaufer's findings suggest a mechanism that may explain some changes in brain connectivity in people with PTSD, for example. One can imagine, she said, that PTSD patients could develop a stronger connectivity between the hippocampus and the amygdala—the seat of the brain's fight or flight response—and lower than normal connectivity between the hippocampus and prefrontal cortex, which moderates our responses.

"You can imagine that if your amygdala and hippocampus are better connected, that could mean that your fear responses are much quicker, which is something you see in stress survivors," she said. "On the other hand, if your connections are not so good to the prefrontal cortex, your ability to shut down responses is impaired. So, when you are in a stressful situation, the inhibitory pathways from the prefrontal cortex telling you not to get stressed don't work as well as the amygdala shouting to the hippocampus, 'This is terrible!' You have a much bigger response than you should."

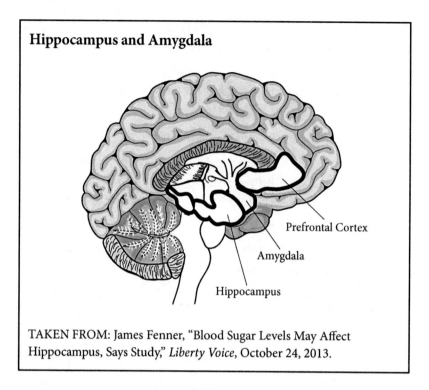

Hippocampus and Amygdala

Prefrontal Cortex

Amygdala

Hippocampus

TAKEN FROM: James Fenner, "Blood Sugar Levels May Affect Hippocampus, Says Study," *Liberty Voice*, October 24, 2013.

She is involved in a study to test this hypothesis in PTSD patients, and continues to study brain changes in rodents subjected to chronic stress or to adverse environments in early life.

Stress Tweaks Stem Cells

Kaufer's lab, which conducts research on the molecular and cellular effects of acute and chronic stress, focused in this study on neural stem cells in the hippocampus of the brains of adult rats. These stem cells were previously thought to mature only into neurons or a type of glial cell called an astrocyte. The researchers found, however, that chronic stress also made stem cells in the hippocampus mature into another type of glial cell called an oligodendrocyte, which produces the myelin that sheaths nerve cells.

The finding, which they demonstrated in rats and cultured rat brain cells, suggests a key role for oligodendrocytes in long-term and perhaps permanent changes in the brain that could set the stage for later mental problems. Oligodendrocytes also help form synapses—sites where one cell talks to another—and help control the growth pathway of axons, which make those synapse connections.

The fact that chronic stress also decreases the number of stem cells that mature into neurons could provide an explanation for how chronic stress also affects learning and memory, she said.

Kaufer is now conducting experiments to determine how stress in infancy affects the brain's white matter, and whether chronic early-life stress decreases resilience later in life. She also is looking at the effects of therapies, ranging from exercise to antidepressant drugs, that reduce the impact of stress and stress hormones.

| "*Even within mainstream psychiatry, few continue to argue that the increase in mental illness is due to previous underdiagnosis of mental disorders.*"

Mental Illness Is Overdiagnosed

Bruce Levine

Bruce Levine is a clinical psychologist in Cincinnati, Ohio, and the author of Surviving America's Depression Epidemic. *In the following viewpoint, he argues that there has been a huge increase in mental illness diagnoses over the past few years. He attributes this to several factors. First, doctors are overdiagnosing normal sadness and distress as mental illness. Second, he says, antipsychotic medications can actually worsen mental illness in many cases, resulting in more and more severe diagnoses. Finally, he argues that American culture is isolating and alienating, causing people to withdraw into depression or other conditions that are diagnosed as mental illnesses.*

As you read, consider the following questions:

1. What did Martin Seligman identify as "two astonishing things about the rate of depression" across the twentieth century, according to the viewpoint?

2. According to Levine, what percentage of workers are engaged with their jobs according to the 2013 Gallup survey?

3. Under what circumstances do those with ADHD do worst, according to Levine?

In "The Epidemic of Mental Illness: Why?" (*New York Review of Books*, 2011), Marcia Angell, former editor in chief of the *New England Journal of Medicine*, discusses overdiagnosis of psychiatric disorders, pathologizing of normal behaviors, Big Pharma [referring to the pharmaceutical industry] corruption of psychiatry, and the adverse effects of psychiatric medications. While diagnostic expansionism and Big Pharma certainly deserve a large share of the blame for this epidemic, there is another reason.

A June 2013 Gallup poll revealed that 70% of Americans hate their jobs or have "checked out" of them. Life may or may not suck any more than it did a generation ago, but our belief in "progress" has increased expectations that life should be more satisfying, resulting in mass disappointment. For many of us, society has become increasingly alienating, isolating, and insane, and earning a buck means more degrees, compliance, ass-kissing, shit-eating, and inauthenticity. So, we want to rebel. However, many of us feel hopeless about the possibility of either our own escape from societal oppression or that political activism can create societal change. So, many of us, especially young Americans, rebel by what is commonly called mental illness.

While historically some Americans have consciously faked mental illness to rebel from oppressive societal demands—e.g., a young Malcolm X acted crazy to successfully avoid military service—today, the vast majority of Americans who are diagnosed and treated for mental illness are in no way proud malingerers in the fashion of Malcolm X. Many of us, sadly, are ashamed of our inefficiency and nonproductivity and desperately try to fit in. However, try as we might to pay attention, adapt, adjust, and comply with our alienating jobs, boring schools, and sterile society, our humanity gets in the way, and we become anxious, depressed, and dysfunctional.

The Mental Illness Epidemic

Severe, disabling mental illness has dramatically increased in the United States. Marcia Angell, in her 2011 *New York Review of Books* piece, summarizes: "The tally of those who are so disabled by mental disorders that they qualify for Supplemental Security Income (SSI) or Social Security Disability Insurance (SSDI) increased nearly two and a half times between 1987 and 2007—from 1 in 184 Americans to 1 in 76. For children, the rise is even more startling—a thirty-five-fold increase in the same two decades."

Angell also reports that a large survey of adults conducted between 2001 and 2003 sponsored by the National Institute of Mental Health found that at some point in their lives, 46% of Americans met the criteria established by the American Psychiatric Association for at least one mental illness.

In 1998, Martin Seligman, then president of the American Psychological Association, spoke to the National Press Club about an American depression epidemic: "We discovered two astonishing things about the rate of depression across the century. The first was there is now between ten and twenty times as much of it as there was fifty years ago. And the second is that it has become a young person's problem. When I first started working in depression thirty years ago . . . the average age at which the first onset of depression occurred was 29.5. . . . Now the average age is between 14 and 15."

In 2011, the U.S. Centers for Disease Control and Prevention (CDC) reported that antidepressant use in the United States has increased nearly 400% in the last two decades, making antidepressants the most frequently used class of medications by Americans ages 18–44 years. By 2008, 23% of women ages 40–59 years were taking antidepressants.

The CDC, on May 3, 2013, reported that the suicide rate among Americans ages 35–64 years increased 28.4% between 1999 and 2010 (from 13.7 suicides per 100,000 population in 1999 to 17.6 per 100,000 in 2010).

The *New York Times* reported in 2007 that the number of American children and adolescents treated for bipolar disorder had increased 40-fold between 1994 and 2003. In May 2013, the CDC reported in "Mental Health Surveillance Among Children—United States, 2005–2011," the following: "A total of 13%–20% of children living in the United States experience a mental disorder in a given year, and surveillance during 1994–2011 has shown the prevalence of these conditions to be increasing."

Overdiagnosis, Pathologizing the Normal, and Psychiatric Drug Adverse Effects

Even within mainstream psychiatry, few continue to argue that the increase in mental illness is due to previous underdiagnosis of mental disorders. The most common explanations for the mental illness epidemic include recent overdiagnosis of psychiatric disorders, diagnostic expansionism, and psychiatry's pathologizing normal behavior.

The first *DSM* (short for *Diagnostic and Statistical Manual of Mental Disorders*), psychiatry's diagnostic "bible," was published by the American Psychiatric Association in 1952 and listed 106 disorders (initially called "reactions"). *DSM-II* was published in 1968, and the number of disorders increased to 182. *DSM-III* was published in 1980, and though homosexuality was dropped from it, diagnoses were expanded to 265, with several child disorders added that would soon become popular, including oppositional defiant disorder (ODD). *DSM-IV*, published in 1994, contained 365 diagnoses.

DSM-5 was published in May 2013. The journal *PLOS Medicine* reported in 2012, "69% of the *DSM-5* task force members report having ties to the pharmaceutical industry." *DSM-5* did not add as many new diagnoses as had previous revisions. However, *DSM-5* has been criticized even by some mainstream psychiatrists such as Allen Frances, the former chair of the *DSM-IV* task force, for creating more mental patients by making it easier to qualify for a mental illness, especially for depression (see Frances's "Last Plea to DSM-5: Save Grief from the Drug Companies").

In the last two decades, there have been a slew of books written by journalists and mental health professionals about the lack of science behind the *DSM*, the overdiagnosis of psychiatric disorders, and the pathologizing of normal behaviors. A sample of these books include Paula Caplan's *They Say You're Crazy* (1995); Herb Kutchins and Stuart Kirk's *Making Us Crazy* (1997); Allan Horwitz and Jerome Wakefield's *The Loss of Sadness: How Psychiatry Transformed Normal Sorrow into Depressive Disorder* (2007); Christopher Lane's *Shyness: How Normal Behavior Became a Sickness* (2008); Stuart Kirk, Tomi Gomory, and David Cohen's *Mad Science: Psychiatric Coercion, Diagnosis, and Drugs* (2013); Gary Greenberg's *The Book of Woe: The DSM and the Unmaking of Psychiatry* (2013); and Allen Frances's *Saving Normal* (2013).

Even more remarkable than former chair of the *DSM-IV* task force, Allen Frances, jumping on the *DSM*-trashing bandwagon has been the harsh critique of *DSM-5* by Thomas Insel, director of the National Institute of Mental Health (NIMH). Insel recently announced that the *DSM*'s diagnostic categories lack validity, and that "NIMH will be re-orienting its research away from *DSM* categories." And psychiatrist Robert Spitzer, former chair of the *DSM-III* task force, wrote the foreword to Horwitz and Wakefield's *The Loss of Sadness* and is now critical of *DSM*'s inattention to context in which the symptoms occur which, he points out, can medicalize normal experiences.

So, in just two decades, pointing out the pseudoscience of the *DSM* has gone from being an "extremist slur of radical anti-psychiatrists" to a mainstream proposition from the former chairs of both the *DSM-III* and *DSM-IV* task forces and the director of NIMH.

Yet another explanation for the epidemic may also be evolving from radical to mainstream, thanks primarily to the efforts of investigative journalist Robert Whitaker and his book *Anatomy of an Epidemic* (2010). Whitaker argues that the adverse effects of psychiatric medications are the primary cause of the epidemic. He reports that these drugs, for many patients, cause episodic and moderate emotional and behavioral problems to become severe, chronic, and disabling ones.

Examining the scientific literature that now extends over 50 years, Whitaker discovered that while some psychiatric medications for some people may be effective over the short term, these drugs increase the likelihood that a person will become chronically ill over the long term. Whitaker reports, "The scientific literature shows that many patients treated for a milder problem will worsen in response to a drug—say have a manic episode after taking an antidepressant—and that can lead to a new and more severe diagnosis like bipolar disorder."

With respect to the dramatic increase of pediatric bipolar disorder, Whitaker points out that, "Once psychiatrists started putting 'hyperactive' children on Ritalin, they started to see prepubertal children with manic symptoms. Same thing happened when psychiatrists started prescribing antidepressants to children and teenagers. A significant percentage had manic or hypomanic reactions to the antidepressants." And then these children and teenagers are put on heavier-duty drugs, including drug cocktails, often do not respond favorably to treatment, and deteriorate. And that, for Whitaker, is a major reason for the thirty-five-fold increase between 1987 and 2007 of children classified as being disabled by mental disorders. (See my 2010 interview with him, "Are Prozac and Other Psychiatric Drugs Causing the Astonishing Rise of Mental Illness in America?")

Whitaker's explanation for the epidemic has now, even within mainstream psychiatric institutions, entered into the debate; for example, Whitaker was invited by the National Alliance on Mental Illness (NAMI) to speak at their 2013 annual convention that took place last June. While Whitaker concludes that psychiatry's drug-based paradigm of care is the primary cause of the epidemic, he does not rule out the possibility that various cultural factors may also be contributing to the increase in the number of mentally ill.

Mental Illness as Rebellion Against Society

> The most deadly criticism one could make of modern civilization is that apart from its man-made crises and catastrophes, is not humanly interesting. . . . In the end, such a civilization can produce only a mass man: incapable of spontaneous, self-directed activities: at best patient, docile, disciplined to monotonous work to an almost pathetic degree. . . .
>
> Ultimately such a society produces only two groups of men: the conditioners and the conditioned, the active and passive barbarians.
>
> —Lewis Mumford, 1951

Once it was routine for many respected social critics such as Lewis Mumford and Erich Fromm to express concern about the impact of modern civilization on our mental health. But today the idea that the mental illness epidemic is also being caused by a peculiar rebellion against a dehumanizing society has been, for the most part, removed from the mainstream map. When a societal problem grows to become all-encompassing, we often no longer even notice it.

We are today disengaged from our jobs and our schooling. Young people are pressured to accrue increasingly large student loan debt so as to acquire the credentials to get a job, often one which they will have little enthusiasm about. And increasing numbers of us are completely socially isolated, having nobody who cares about us.

Returning to that June 2013 Gallup survey, "State of the American Workplace: Employee Engagement [Insights for U.S. Business Leaders]," only 30% of workers "were engaged or involved in, enthusiastic about, and committed to their workplace." In contrast to this "actively engaged group," 50% were "not engaged," simply going through the motions to get a paycheck, while 20% were classified as "actively disengaged," hating going to work, and putting energy into undermining their workplace. Those with higher education levels reported more discontent with their workplace.

How engaged are we with our schooling? Another Gallup poll, "The School Cliff: Student Engagement Drops with Each School Year" (released in January 2013), reported that the longer students stay in school, the less engaged they become. The poll surveyed nearly 500,000 students in 37 states in 2012, and found nearly 80% of elementary students reported being engaged with school, but by high school, only 40% reported being engaged. As the pollsters point out, "If we were doing right by our students and our future, these numbers would be the absolute opposite. For each year a student progresses in school, they should be more engaged, not less."

Life clearly sucks more than it did a generation ago when it comes to student loan debt. According to American Student Assistance's "Student Debt Loan Statistics," approximately 37 million Americans have student loan debt. The majority of borrowers still paying back their loans are in their 30s or older. Approximately two-thirds of students graduate college with some education debt. Nearly 30% of college students who take out loans drop out of school, and students who drop out of college before earning a degree struggle most with student loans. As of October 2012, the average amount of student loan debt for the Class of 2011 was $26,600, a 5% increase from 2010. Only about 37% of federal student loan borrowers between 2004 and 2009 managed to make timely payments without postponing payments or becoming delinquent.

Isolation

In addition to the pain of jobs, school, and debt, there is increasingly more pain of social isolation. A major study reported in the *American Sociological Review* in 2006, "Social Isolation in America: Changes in Core Discussion Networks Over Two Decades," examined Americans' core network of *confidants* (those people in our lives we consider close enough to trust with personal information and whom we rely on as a sounding board). Authors reported that in 1985, 10% of Americans said that they had no confidants in their lives; but by 2004, 25% of Americans stated they had no confidants in their lives. This study confirmed the continuation of trends that came to public attention in sociologist Robert Putnam's 2000 book *Bowling Alone*.

Underlying many of psychiatry's nearly 400 diagnoses is the experience of helplessness, hopelessness, passivity, boredom, fear, isolation, and dehumanization—culminating in a loss of autonomy and community connectedness. Do our societal institutions promote:

Enthusiasm—or passivity?

Respectful personal relationships—or manipulative impersonal ones?

Community, trust, and confidence—or isolation, fear, and paranoia?

Empowerment—or helplessness?

Autonomy (self-direction)—or heteronomy (institutional direction)?

Participatory democracy—or authoritarian hierarchies?

Diversity and stimulation—or homogeneity and boredom?

Research (that I documented in *Commonsense Rebellion*) shows that those labeled with attention-deficit/hyperactivity disorder (ADHD) do worst in environments that are boring, repetitive, and externally controlled; and that ADHD-labeled children are indistinguishable from "normals" when they have chosen their learning activities and are interested in them. Thus, the standard classroom could not be more *imperfectly* designed to meet the learning needs of young people who are labeled with ADHD.

Refusal to Comply

As I discussed last year on AlterNet, in "Would We Have Drugged Up Einstein? How Anti-Authoritarianism Is Deemed a Mental Health Problem," there is a fundamental bias in mental health professionals for interpreting inattention and noncompliance as a mental disorder. Those with extended schooling have lived for many years in a world where all pay attention to much that is unstimulating. In this world, one routinely complies with the demands of authorities. Thus for many MDs and PhDs, people who rebel against this attentional and behavioral compliance appear to be from another world—a diagnosable one.

The reality is that with enough helplessness, hopelessness, passivity, boredom, fear, isolation, and dehumanization, we rebel and refuse to comply. Some of us rebel by becoming inattentive. Others become aggressive. In large numbers we eat, drink, and gamble too much. Still others become addicted to drugs—illicit and prescription. Millions work slavishly at dissatisfying jobs, become depressed and passive-aggressive, while no small number of us can't cut it and become homeless and appear crazy. Feeling misunderstood and uncared about, millions of us ultimately rebel against societal demands; however, given our wherewithal, our rebellions are often passive and disorganized, and routinely futile and self-destructive.

When we have hope, energy, and friends, we can choose to rebel against societal oppression with, for example, a wildcat strike or a back-to-the-land commune. But when we lack hope, energy, and friends, we routinely rebel without consciousness of rebellion and in a manner in which we today commonly call mental illness.

For some Americans, no doubt, the conscious goal is to get classified as mentally disabled so as to receive disability payments (averaging $700 to 1,400 per month). But isn't that, too, a withdrawal of cooperation from society and a rebellion of sorts, based on the judgment that this is the best-paying and least-miserable financial option?

"Psychiatric illnesses could be just as common as medical illnesses, especially if they can be minor and do not always require treatment."

That Mental Illness Is Common Does Not Mean It Is Overdiagnosed

Brent Michael Kious

Brent Michael Kious is a psychiatrist and a faculty member at the University of Utah. In the following viewpoint, he argues that mental illnesses may be common yet still be real medical conditions. He points out that conditions such as heart disease and the common cold occur frequently, but they are still real diseases. Even if mental illness is socially caused, or is a reaction to societal factors, he says, that does not mean mental illness is overdiagnosed.

As you read, consider the following questions:

1. What is the prevalence of heart disease in the United States, according to Kious?

Brent Michael Kious, "Must Mental Illness Be Uncommon?," Psychiatrictimes.com, January 30, 2012. © 2012 Psychiatric Times. All rights reserved. Reproduced with permission.

2. Why might doctors want to avoid a diagnosis of mental illness for practical considerations, in Kious's view?

3. By Kious's definition, what is radical pluralism?

It is common for critics of psychiatry to point to the growing prevalence of mental illness as evidence of something wrong. In two essays in the *New York Review of Books*, Dr. Marcia Angell presents several criticisms of psychiatry with this theme. She notes that over the past several decades, the prevalence of mental illness in the United States has skyrocketed. The rate at which mental illness is diagnosed in children has increased by a factor of 35, 10% of 10-year-old boys have ADHD [attention-deficit/hyperactivity disorder] and the lifetime prevalence of mental disorders in the United States is currently 46%. She concludes that there must be some nefarious influence at work, and it seems to her that a cabal of pharmaceutical companies is the most likely culprit.

Heart Disease Is Common

Dr. Angell is an influential critic of medicine, and her arguments, like those in the books she reviews, deserve attention. Here I respond to an assumption central to her essays and related critiques. I think many of us take statistics like those above as evidence of something awry in psychiatry because we assume mental illness must be uncommon. In fact, however, there is no good reason to do so.

Start with a comparison between psychiatric and medical illnesses. There is clearly no problem with thinking the latter are common. Consider heart disease. Its lifetime prevalence for men older than 65 in the United States is 31%, and in recent decades, its global prevalence has increased. This is cause for alarm, but not skepticism. Cancer is also distressingly common, and no one doubts that 19% to 23% of people in the United States will die of cancer or that cancer will develop in 44% of all men.

Neither of the usual theories of mental illnesses suggests they should be different from non-mental illnesses. If mental illnesses are merely brain problems, high prevalence should be unsurprising: The brain is a fabulously complex organ, and complex organs are likely to break down. If instead mental illness cannot be fully understood without reference to a patient's subjective experiences, then high prevalence is still expected, since the trauma and stress that predispose to mental illness are highly prevalent. What, then, occasions our doubt?

There are probably a number of interrelated considerations. First, we may tend to think of mental illness in terms of archetypes such as schizophrenia. Schizophrenia is a chronic and debilitating illness. It is also relatively uncommon, with a lifetime prevalence of 0.5%. If one supposed all mental illnesses were like schizophrenia—lifelong pathological states undermining a person's very identity—then it *would* be surprising if someone said that mental illnesses are common: Most of us are doing okay, most of the time.

Of course, there is no reason to assume all mental illness is akin to schizophrenia. One could be mentally ill both briefly and mildly, without thoroughgoing upheaval of one's life. We accept the existence of medical illnesses such as the common cold. Perhaps we should expect they have mental analogues, and that the latter can be common.

Mental Illness as Common Cold

The skeptic may worry that expanding our nosology to encompass mental analogues of the common cold would render abnormal what we ought to regard as perfectly normal (i.e., acceptable) distress. This concern is superficially compelling, but also confused. Presumably, one problem with classifying "normal" distress as pathological is that it seems to demand treatment. In fact, however, not every medical illness is treated or treatable. The common cold is again an example, but no one thinks it is not a real illness or that it is overdiagnosed.

A related concern might pertain to unnecessary stigma. The label of mental illness entails significant social costs and should not be used without good reason. A diagnosis of ADHD might impair a child's self-esteem and affect his educational, social, and occupational performance. But we should not confuse practical considerations with classificatory ones: how things are, and so how they ought to be classified, is one matter; how we ought to comport ourselves as classifiers is another. Occasionally, someone might be better off not knowing that he or she has cancer or HIV infection. But in neither case does this void the diagnosis.

Skeptics may also share concerns that animated the antipsychiatry movement of the 1960s and 1970s, which argued that psychiatry relied on dubious normative judgments. To be fair, many psychiatric diagnoses probably contain a normative element. This should give us pause, since normativity can easily go awry: The norms driving the diagnosis of *drapetomania* (a slave's desire to flee his master) or the *DSM*'s [*Diagnostic and Statistical Manual of Mental Disorders*] early inclusion of homosexuality were unquestionably wrong. Still, such cases do not show that all psychiatric diagnoses are corrupt, since not all norms are corrupt. Many of the norms implicit in psychiatric diagnoses (such as schizophrenia and other psychotic disorders) are not even *moral* ones, but rather norms of reasoning and inference. And though some might claim that delusional or paranoid beliefs merely constitute "another way of thinking" as good as any other, we need not take those claims seriously.

To be sure, many diagnoses rely on norms that are moral. We might diagnose major depression in a suicidal person and treat him accordingly, and our diagnosis may be independent of any problems with his reasoning, as distinct from problems with his motivations. How we treat him therefore depends on a judgment about how his life should go, which is surely moral.

Moral Judgments

But is reliance on moral judgments a problem per se? For this to be true, what we might call *radical pluralism* would need to be true. Radical pluralism entails that there are no moral requirements extending to behavior that substantially affects only the individual. The anti-psychiatrist thinks many psychiatric diagnoses invoke such requirements, so if radical pluralism is true, such diagnoses are unfounded.

The problem, however, is that radical pluralism is false: Moral judgments about others' self-regarding behavior can be correct. It is easy to say for the sake of argument that we have no grounds for judgments about how others should live, that all such questions are matters of preference. But outside of psychiatry, we make a wide variety of judgments about what others do. As a society, we require persons to refrain from using certain recreational drugs and to do things such as wear their seat belts. The claim that the underlying judgments are necessarily false is too costly if the only payoff is maintaining a radical critique of psychiatry.

We also make decisions for persons who are unable to make decisions for themselves (e.g., young children, adults with dementia). For such "incompetent" persons, the good is not always a matter of preference. But if there are facts about "incompetent" persons' good, similar facts should hold for competent persons. Competence is a matter of having knowledge, understanding that knowledge, and using the knowledge to reason well. If these criteria do not invoke facts about the good, then nothing about competence should make a person more capable of determining his good than the incompetent person. And if the criteria *do* invoke facts about the good, then such facts exist. Either way, radical pluralism is in trouble.

Finally, skeptics may worry that mental illnesses are socially constructed. There are several senses in which this may be true, but none of them clearly suggests mental illnesses are uncommon. One way things can be socially constructed is for their existence to depend on social practices, just as chess games and the Rose Parade are social constructs. Some mental illnesses, such as anorexia nervosa, may be constructed in this fashion. But being the product of social conditions does not make something unreal: The Rose Parade is clearly real, even if it is not natural. Similarly, medical conditions such as mesothelioma [a cancer caused by exposure to asbestos] are real, even though they would not occur but for some social practices. Being socially constructed in this sense should not, therefore, impugn the reality of mental illnesses.

Sometimes social construction is a matter of applying arbitrary categories to natural continua. Some think race is socially constructed in this way: Variations in skin tone, hair color, and the like are real, but identified races correspond to no natural divisions. Our color categories are similarly constructed: Color phenomena comprise continuous spectra onto which we impose divisions, which vary somewhat from culture to culture and which are not natural. But, again, being non-natural does not entail being unreal: No one would seriously contend that *redness* is not real, or that we should disband our use of that concept.

Looping

Finally, things can be socially constructed insofar as they are what [Ian] Hacking called looping kinds: The phenomena categorized change over time because people's behavior changes in response to the categories. Mental illness can obviously be like this, but it is again no mark against reality. Most cultural categories loop. The promulgation of the notion of *hippie culture* in the 1960s probably led more people to become hippies. But no one supposes that hippies were not *really* hippies. The kind looped, but remained real.

To conclude, I should emphasize that I am not trying to argue that mental illness really *is* common, which is partly an empirical matter. Nor am I concerned with defending the legitimacy of the entire corpus of psychiatric diagnoses, many of which could be spurious or overused. My aim instead has been to show that our resistance to the potential ubiquity of mental illness is not a priori justified. Psychiatric illnesses could be just as common as medical illnesses, especially if they can be minor and do not always require treatment. Dr. Angell and others may be right to claim that we should be concerned about the current practice of psychiatry. But the simple fact that mental illnesses seem to be common is not one of them.

Periodical and Internet Sources Bibliography

The following articles have been selected to supplement the diverse views presented in this chapter.

Victoria A. Brownworth	"Crazy Every Day: America's Mental Illness Epidemic," *Huffington Post*, October 7, 2013.
John M. Grohol	"A Mental Illness Epidemic? Or Hype Masquerading as Journalism?," Psych Central, August 28, 2013.
Clyde Haberman	"Debate Persists over Diagnosing Mental Health Disorders, Long After 'Sybil,'" *New York Times*, November 23, 2014.
Thomas R. Insel, Pamela Y. Collins, and Steven E. Hyman	"Darkness Invisible: The Hidden Global Costs of Mental Illness," *Foreign Affairs*, January–February 2015.
Marissa Maldonado	"How Stress Affects Mental Health," Psych Central, February 25, 2014.
David Mills	"Scientists May Have Solved the Mystery of What Causes Schizophrenia," HealthlineNews, May 4, 2015.
Alexander Nazaryan	"When Will Mental Illness Finally Yield to Science?," *Newsweek*, August 11, 2014.
Jesse Singal	"America's Epidemic of Psychiatric Over-Diagnosis," Daily Beast, June 21, 2013.
Christina Sterbenz	"The Way We Diagnose Mental Illness Might Be a 'Mistake,'" Business Insider, November 8, 2013.
Katie Waldeck	"7 Major Links Between Diet and Mental Health," Care2.com, April 23, 2015.

CHAPTER 2

How Should Mental Illness Be Treated?

Chapter Preface

Mental illness is often treated with pharmaceuticals or therapy. However, there is another, increasingly popular treatment option: cell phone applications.

Cell phone apps can provide those with mental illness with a way to schedule, monitor, and organize their day-to-day lives that can help control and manage their mental illness. For example, the Recovery Record app, developed by psychologist Jenna Tregarthen, reminds people with eating disorders when to eat and provides simple rewards (a puzzle piece, positive encouragement) when they have a meal. The app Operation Reach Out was developed by the military as a way to reduce suicide; it provides videos and data so that users can assess their mental state and features links to resources so they can get help if needed. Other apps teach relaxation techniques, or help track symptoms of depression.

Mental health apps can be therapeutic, and many users report finding them helpful. They also hold great promise for reducing health care costs, since apps are very cheap compared to doctors' visits. One promising app, called PRIORI (Predicting Individual Outcomes for Rapid Intervention), is designed to give those with bipolar disorder an early warning of when manic or depressive episodes are imminent. The app analyzes the patient's voice; if the voice is fast, a manic episode may be about to occur. If the voice is slow, there may be a danger of depression. A March 2015 article for Al Jazeera said researchers at the University of Michigan hope the app can help doctors and patients better control bipolar conditions. Melvin McInnis, the lead psychiatrist on PRIORI, said, "The app has one goal, to help people with bipolar disorder. The holy grail is to prevent an episode and improve the quality of life."

However, there are some concerns as well. For many with mental health issues, privacy is very important; some critics worry that apps that track data may be hacked, releasing sensitive information. Some also worry that the mental health apps are not subjected to rigorous testing, and so may not be as beneficial as advertised. Apps that are funded by the National Institute of Mental Health must be tested and peer reviewed, but other apps do not necessarily have to be, and may promise more than they deliver.

The following chapter looks at other treatments for mental illness, including pharmaceuticals and therapy as well as raising public awareness of conditions such as post-traumatic stress disorder and male suicide.

> "Successful treatment for schizophrenia is comprehensive and includes both pharmacological and psychosocial interventions."

Pharmaceuticals Are Central to the Treatment of Schizophrenia

Margarita Tartakovsky

Margarita Tartakovsky is an associate editor at Psych Central. In the following viewpoint, she discusses how to treat schizophrenia. She says that successful treatment involves several elements. This usually includes medication and a longtime collaboration with a doctor to make sure the medications are taken as prescribed. Treatment can also include therapeutic interventions, treatment for other problems such as drug addiction, and peer counseling.

As you read, consider the following questions:

1. According to the author, what is the most common reason that people with schizophrenia stop taking their medication?

2. What does Tartakovsky say is the most common co-occurring disorder for people with schizophrenia, and how can it be addressed?

3. According to the viewpoint, what forms can peer counseling for schizophrenia take?

Schizophrenia is a complex and often chronic illness that requires long-term treatment. Medication is the bedrock of managing schizophrenia, said Peter Buckley, MD, a psychiatrist and expert in schizophrenia, and dean of the Medical College of Georgia at Georgia Regents University.

But a comprehensive plan, which includes familial support and education, and considers the person's individual psychological needs, is key, he said.

The specifics of treatment depend on the stage of the illness and the person's age, said Robert Buchanan, MD, director of the Maryland Psychiatric Research Center and a leading expert in schizophrenia. "Someone who is having a first episode of psychosis might have a different treatment plan than someone who is 45 and has been ill for many years."

"The most effective way to treat the illness is for the person to learn about the disorder and its symptoms, and to take an active role in their treatment," said Susan Gingerich, MSW, a clinician based in Philadelphia with over 30 years of experience working with individuals with schizophrenia and their families.

That includes focusing on life goals that are important to you, such as working, going to school or having close relationships, she said.

It also includes other key elements: taking medication as prescribed; learning to manage stress and symptoms; avoiding drugs and alcohol; developing and using a relapse prevention plan; sticking with treatment; and building a social support network, she said.

Taking Medication

Because schizophrenia tends to be a lifelong illness, it requires lifelong management with medication. Finding the right medication is a trial-and-error process. "There are no predicators for which drug will be most effective for a particular individual," Buchanan said. That's why having a collaborative relationship with the prescribing physician is so important.

Medication adherence is a big challenge. In the Clinical Antipsychotic Trials of Intervention Effectiveness (CATIE), 74 percent of patients stopped taking their medication within the first 18 months of treatment. Not taking medication increases the risk for relapse, hospitalization and suicidal behavior.

"Adherence seems very simple, but it's actually remarkably complicated," Buckley said. The reasons people don't take their medication differ with each individual, he said. The most common reason is lack of awareness of being ill. As Buckley said, if you don't consider yourself psychotic, why would you take an antipsychotic medication?

There are gradients of insight, and insight may fluctuate, Buchanan said. For instance, "a person may not have insight into their illness, per say, but they may know that they're having trouble going outside of their house and feeling comfortable." In supportive therapy, the therapist and patient may talk about how medication can help them achieve their goal of feeling comfortable with leaving their house, he said.

Individuals also might not take medication because it doesn't work or has bothersome side effects. Substance abuse is common, and may contribute to non-adherence, as well.

Other factors include the disapproving opinions of family members and others' bad experiences with medication, Buckley said.

Plus, "lots of people don't take their medicines exactly as prescribed." For instance, individuals who've been taking blood pressure medication for many years also slip up, he said.

According to Buchanan, a collaborative relationship between the psychiatrist and patient is critical in enhancing adherence. In fact, another reason people don't take medication is because they feel pressured or "ordered" to take it "without having been involved in shared decision making," said Gingerich, also coauthor of *The Complete Family Guide to Schizophrenia, Social Skills Training for Schizophrenia,* and *Illness Management and Recovery: Personalized Skills and Strategies for Those with Mental Illness.*

It's important to have open discussions around what the patient finds helpful about the medication and what they don't like, Buchanan said. This way they can make adjustments and try different medications, he said.

Sometimes, people don't like taking pills or because of their cognitive impairment, they have a hard time remembering to take their medication, Buchanan said. One strategy is to incorporate medication into the person's daily routine, Gingerich said.

For instance, this can include "putting one's pill bottle next to their tooth brush so they are reminded to take their medication when they brush their teeth," along with using pill organizers and setting up cues "such as using a calendar, or programming one's cell phone."

Another strategy is "offering the option of long-acting injectable medication. Instead of taking a pill every day, [patients] can receive a shot once every two weeks or four weeks," Buchanan said.

Psychosocial Interventions

"Psychosocial interventions are a cornerstone of the comprehensive treatment of patients with schizophrenia, and when used in combination with medication, they are more effective than antipsychotics alone," write Buckley and Brian Miller, MD, PhD, in the 2013 edition of *Conn's Current Therapy.*

Causes of Schizophrenia

Scientists have long known that schizophrenia runs in families. The illness occurs in 1 percent of the general population, but it occurs in 10 percent of people who have a first-degree relative with the disorder, such as a parent, brother, or sister. People who have second-degree relatives (aunts, uncles, grandparents, or cousins) with the disease also develop schizophrenia more often than the general population. The risk is highest for an identical twin of a person with schizophrenia. He or she has a 40 to 65 percent chance of developing the disorder.

We inherit our genes from both parents. Scientists believe several genes are associated with an increased risk of schizophrenia, but that no gene causes the disease by itself. In fact, recent research has found that people with schizophrenia tend to have higher rates of rare genetic mutations. These genetic differences involve hundreds of different genes and probably disrupt brain development.

Other recent studies suggest that schizophrenia may result in part when a certain gene that is key to making important brain chemicals malfunctions. This problem may affect the part of the brain involved in developing higher-functioning skills. Research into this gene is ongoing, so it is not yet possible to use the genetic information to predict who will develop the disease.

"What Is Schizophrenia?,"
National Institute of Mental Health.

This can include educating families about schizophrenia and the best ways to offer support. Having loved ones involved in treatment can increase medication adherence and decrease relapse rates.

Other interventions include social skills training, which teaches individuals with schizophrenia to be assertive, resolve conflict and navigate work issues.

Supported employment helps people find and keep jobs in the community based on their abilities and preferences. It includes "individually tailored job development, rapid job search, availability of ongoing job supports, and integration of vocational and mental health services," according to [a] 2009 research-based summary of psychosocial treatments. Supported employment helps in building self-esteem and self-image, Buchanan said.

Cognitive behavioral therapy (CBT) aims to treat the positive symptoms of schizophrenia, such as hallucinations and delusions, and negative symptoms, such as lack of motivation. It also helps individuals identify their recovery goals and work toward them. And it helps with any co-occurring disorders such as depression and anxiety.

Substance abuse is the most common co-occurring disorder for people with schizophrenia. When a person has both schizophrenia and issues with substance use, "it is important to get treatment from professionals who treat the disorders concurrently and in an integrated way," Gingerich said.

This treatment is typically called "integrated treatment for dual disorders" or "co-occurring disorder treatment."

According to Gingerich, it usually includes these areas: helping the person identify why they are using substances (for instance, it might be to cope with symptoms); talking about how they can get these same needs met without turning to drugs or alcohol; helping them identify the harmful consequences of their use, such as relapse or legal or relationship problems; "helping the person weigh the pros and cons of sobriety"; and "identifying high-risk situations and ways to avoid them or cope with them."

It also includes helping the person make a plan for reducing their use or stopping it altogether, when they're ready, she said. And it includes gathering support, "from groups such as Dual Recovery Anonymous and from sober friends and family."

Other Interventions

Peer counseling can be very helpful and take various forms. It tends to be similar to Alcoholics Anonymous, as individuals who are living successfully with schizophrenia are trained to help others with the illness. They may help with everything from sharing insight into navigating the mental health care system to providing information on managing stress and symptoms.

You can learn more about peer services and support at the National Alliance on Mental Illness.

Antipsychotic medication doesn't help with the debilitating cognitive deficits schizophrenia causes, which affect nearly all patients. That's why researchers also are exploring the efficacy of cognitive remediation.

This is a behavioral training-based intervention that aims to improve cognitive processes, such as attention, memory and executive function. Most cognitive remediation programs use computers and target one or several cognitive skills.

Often, it's the cognitive symptoms that are most damaging to a person's ability to work, study and even live independently. Cognitive deficits make it harder to remember and process information. Individuals may have a difficult time with everything from remembering their supervisor's instructions to maintaining a budget to navigating public transportation....

Again, successful treatment for schizophrenia is comprehensive and includes both pharmacological and psychosocial interventions. Family education is especially critical.

It's also important to have faith in your loved one and "help them keep hope alive," Gingerich said. "Focus on their strengths and talents and how they can accomplish their goals and contribute to the world."

And, if you have schizophrenia, have faith in yourself. "People with schizophrenia can lead productive, rewarding lives."

"Drugs have serious side effects, and at least 50% of patients either refuse or fail to take them."

Psychotherapy May Be an Effective Treatment for Severe Mental Illness

Rachel Pruchno

Rachel Pruchno is a professor of medicine at Rowan University School of Osteopathic Medicine. In the following viewpoint, she argues that there is reason to believe that cognitive behavior therapy (without drugs) can be effective in treating severe psychiatric illnesses. She says that current studies are unclear and more research is needed but that there does seem to be small improvements in mental illness through such therapies. She concludes that better-designed studies are needed, as a continued willingness to consider options other than drug treatment in managing mental illness is becoming more common.

As you read, consider the following questions:

1. What is the first question Pruchno said she asked herself about psychotherapy and mental illness?

Rachel Pruchno, "Is Psychotherapy Effective for Severe Mental Illness?," Psychology today.com, April 2, 2014. © 2014 Psychology Today. All rights reserved. Reproduced with permission.

2. What question does Pruchno say that researchers should perhaps be asking about CBT?

3. According to the viewpoint, what does Jessica Arenella say about the possibility that psychotherapy relies on a placebo effect?

Last week [March 14, 2014], *Science* magazine, a leading journal of original scientific research, global news, and commentary, ran an article entitled "Talking Back to Madness" that made me believe we're finally taking severe mental illness seriously.

Talking Rather than Medicating

The article begins with a story about a man named Terry who started hearing voices that told him to harm himself and his family members at 13 years old. He later became addicted to heroin and his marriage ended in divorce. Terry credits psychotherapist Jessica Arenella, PhD, whom he met when he was 46, with saving his life. For more than a decade, Dr. Arenella has helped Terry follow the gentle voices and ignore the nasty ones.

The article explains how some clinical psychologists are successfully treating psychosis with "talk" psychotherapy. Bucking a decades-old trend in which antipsychotic drugs have been the first line of defense against illnesses such as schizophrenia, they are engaging with patients' symptoms, such as hearing voices or experiencing hallucinations, and taking them seriously.

As a research scientist, the first question I asked myself was, "Is there evidence that psychotherapy works for people with severe mental illness?" I thought I'd find the answer easily, since two meta-analyses examining this issue were published this year. The first, by David Turner and his colleagues, examined the relative efficacy of six different interventions for patients with psychosis. Studying 48 outcome trials that involved 3,295 patients, they concluded that cognitive behavioral therapy (CBT) was significantly more efficacious than other interventions in reducing positive symptoms of psychosis. This finding was robust in all sensitivity analyses for risk of bias, but lost significance in sensitivity analyses for investigator blinding, which the investigators suggest may have been a function of reduced power.

The second meta-analysis, by [S.] Jauhar and colleagues, examined findings from 52 studies. It focused on people with schizophrenia who participated in either CBT or treatment as usual. That analysis concluded that CBT has a therapeutic effect on schizophrenic symptoms in the "small" range, effects that are reduced when sources of bias, particularly masking (treatment group is not hidden from those conducting the assessments), are controlled for.

These investigators note that since 2008, only two published studies found a significant advantage for CBT when overall symptoms were the outcome and only one study found an advantage for CBT when positive symptoms were the outcome. Their conclusion: "The UK government's continued vigorous advocacy of this form of treatment might be considered puzzling."

These meta-analyses and an NIH [National Institutes of Health]–funded study based on 74 people, many of whom dropped out of the study before it ended, published last month in the *Lancet* sparked controversy in the scientific world as well as in social media. There has been a lot of finger-pointing and jumping up and down. Scientists questioning the value of CBT point to the flaws in existing studies, including small samples; high dropout rates; inclusion of people at all phases of illness; failure to blind treatment; outcomes that are not independent of one another; failure to measure treatment dose; and follow-up periods that are too brief. Meanwhile, scientists convinced of the value of CBT counter that the meta-analyses undervalue the efficacy of CBT by unfairly removing studies from consideration, including studies that use different forms of CBT, and failing to control for inclusion and exclusion criteria that can bias study findings.

No Side Effects

Those favoring CBT and those believing it is ineffective for persons with severe mental illness agree about the magnitude of the effect size (a measure of the strength of a finding) in these meta-analyses. The two recent meta-analyses found effect sizes for CBT to be approximately .3—similar in magnitude to that of studies examining the effects of clozapine for controlling psychotic symptoms. But drugs have serious side effects, and at least 50% of patients either refuse or fail to take them. This is not true of CBT.

As a scientist, I have to conclude that we have a long way to go before we understand whether CBT is an effective treatment for people with severe mental illness. We need adequately powered studies that assess proximal as well as distal outcomes. We need more sophisticated study designs in which assessors are blind to treatment status. We need studies with more explicit inclusion and exclusion criteria. And we need studies with designs that replicate one another so that findings are comparable. Maybe researchers have been asking the wrong questions. Maybe the question is not whether CBT is effective, but for whom and when is it effective. The bottom line is we need more high-quality research studies before we know whether or not CBT is effective.

As the mother of an adult child with severe mental illness, I'm delighted to see such controversy roiling the scientists. It means people are passionate about treating mental illness. It means we're looking beyond medications for ways to treat some of our sickest citizens. For now, I have to agree with Jessica Arenella, PhD, the psychologist treating Terry who says, "In the end it doesn't matter whether talk therapies work because of the theory behind them or just because someone is taking the patient and their symptoms seriously. It may be a placebo effect [that is, an effect caused because the patient believes it will work], but I will go for all the placebo effect I can get."

It may be a placebo effect, but Dr. Arenella has seen it work. Maybe someday we'll figure out how to do the science right. And maybe someday someone will figure out how to help my daughter.

> *"Americans wounded in their own neighborhoods are not getting treatment for PTSD. They're not even getting diagnosed."*

Better Treatment Is Needed for Post-Traumatic Stress Disorder

Lois Beckett

Lois Beckett is a reporter for ProPublica, covering the intersection of data, technology, and politics. In the following viewpoint, she reports that people in violent neighborhoods in the United States often develop post-traumatic stress disorder (PTSD). However, trauma centers in the United States often do not screen for PTSD and are ill-equipped to treat the disorder. This leaves many people impaired and unable to work or function properly. It can also lead to more violence, as victims of PTSD may be quick to become angry or overreact to stress. Beckett concludes that more routine screening and treatment for PTSD is needed, especially in high-crime areas where the disorder is common.

As you read, consider the following questions:

1. According to Beckett, what percentage of Americans suffer from PTSD at some point in their lives, and in what areas are those rates higher?

2. According to the viewpoint, why did some people argue that gang members could not get PTSD? Was this argument correct, according to Grant Marshall?

3. According to Beckett, what is Healing Hurt People, and what does it do?

Chicago's Cook County hospital has one of the busiest trauma centers in the nation, treating about 2,000 patients a year for gunshots, stabbings and other violent injuries.

So when researchers started screening patients there for post-traumatic stress disorder [PTSD] in 2011, they assumed they would find cases.

PTSD Is Widespread

They just didn't know how many: Fully 43 percent of the patients they examined—and more than half of gunshot-wound victims—had signs of PTSD.

"We knew these people were going to have PTSD symptoms," said Kimberly Joseph, a trauma surgeon at the hospital. "We didn't know it was going to be as extensive."

What the work showed, Joseph said, is, "This is a much more urgent problem than you think."

Joseph proposed spending about $200,000 a year to add staffers to screen all at-risk patients for PTSD and connect them with treatment. The taxpayer-subsidized hospital has an annual budget of roughly $450 million. But Joseph said hospital administrators turned her down and suggested she look for outside funding. "Right now, we don't have institutional support," said Joseph, who is now applying for outside grants.

A hospital spokeswoman would not comment on why the hospital decided not to pay for regular screening. The hospital is part of a pilot program with other area hospitals to help "pediatrics patients identified with PTSD," said the spokeswoman, Marisa Kollias. "The Cook County Health and Hospitals System is committed to treating all patients with high-quality care." Right now, social workers try to identify patients with the most severe PTSD symptoms, said Carol Reese, the trauma center's violence prevention coordinator and an Episcopal priest.

"I'm not going to tell you we have everything we need in place right now, because we don't," Reese said. "We have a chaplain and a social worker and a couple of social work interns trying to see 5,000 people. We're not staffed to do it."

A growing body of research shows that Americans with traumatic injuries develop PTSD at rates comparable to veterans of war. Just like veterans, civilians can suffer flashbacks, nightmares, paranoia, and social withdrawal. While the United States has been slow to provide adequate treatment to troops affected by post-traumatic stress, the military has made substantial progress in recent years. It now regularly screens for PTSD, works to fight the stigma associated with mental health treatment and educates military families about potential symptoms.

Few similar efforts exist for civilian trauma victims. Americans wounded in their own neighborhoods are not getting treatment for PTSD. They're not even getting diagnosed.

Studies show that, overall, about 8 percent of Americans suffer from PTSD at some point in their lives. But the rates appear to be much higher in communities—such as poor, largely African American pockets of Detroit, Atlanta, Chicago and Philadelphia—where high rates of violent crime have persisted despite a national decline.

Inner Cities Have High PTSD Rates

Researchers in Atlanta interviewed more than 8,000 inner-city residents and found that about two-thirds said they had been violently attacked and that half knew someone who had been murdered. At least 1 in 3 of those interviewed experienced symptoms consistent with PTSD at some point in their lives—and that's a "conservative estimate," said Dr. Kerry Ressler, the lead investigator on the project.

"The rates of PTSD we see are as high or higher than Iraq, Afghanistan or Vietnam veterans," Ressler said. "We have a whole population who is traumatized."

Post-traumatic stress can be a serious burden: It can take a toll on relationships and parenting, lead to family conflict and interfere with jobs. A national study of patients with traumatic injuries found that those who developed post-traumatic stress were less likely to have returned to work a year after their injuries.

It may also have a broader social cost. "Neglect of civilian PTSD as a public health concern may be compromising public safety," Ressler and his coauthors concluded in a 2012 paper.

For most people, untreated PTSD will not lead to violence. But "there's a subgroup of people who are at risk, in the wrong place, at the wrong time, of reacting in a violent way or an aggressive way, that they might not have if they had had their PTSD treated," Ressler said.

Research on military veterans has found that the symptom of "chronic hyperarousal"—the distorted sense of always being under extreme threat—can lead to increased aggression and violent behavior.

"Very minor threats can be experienced, by what the signals in your body tell you, as, 'You're in acute danger,'" said Sandra Bloom, a psychiatrist and former president of the International Society for Traumatic Stress Studies.

Another issue, wrote researchers at Drexel University, is that people with symptoms of PTSD may be more likely to carry a weapon in order to "restore feelings of safety."

Hospital trauma centers, which work on the front lines of neighborhood violence, could help address the lack of treatment. Indeed, the American College of Surgeons [ACS], which sets standards for the care of patients with traumatic injuries, is set to recommend that trauma centers "evaluate, support and treat" patients for post-traumatic stress.

More Screening Needed

But it's not a requirement, and few hospitals appear to be doing it. ProPublica surveyed a top-level trauma center in each of the 21 cities with the nation's highest homicide rates. Just one, the Spirit of Charity Trauma Center in New Orleans, currently screens all seriously injured patients for PTSD. At another, Detroit Receiving Hospital, psychologists talk with injured crime victims about PTSD.

Other hospitals have a patchwork of resources or none at all. At two hospitals, in Birmingham, Alabama, and St. Louis, Missouri, trauma center staff said they hope to institute routine PTSD screening by the end of the year.

Doctors in Baltimore, Newark, Memphis, and Jackson, Miss., said they wanted to do more to address PTSD, but they do not have the money.

They said adding even small amounts to hospital budgets is a hard sell in a tough economic climate. That's especially true at often cash-strapped public hospitals.

In order to add a staff member to screen and follow up on PTSD, "Do I lay someone else off in another area?" asked Carnell Cooper, a trauma surgeon at [R Adams Cowley] Shock Trauma [Center] in Baltimore.

Many public hospitals rely on state Medicaid programs to cover treatment of low-income patients. But several surgeons across the country said they did not know of any way they could bill Medicaid for screenings.

The federal government often provides guidance to state Medicaid programs on best practices for patient care and how to fund them. But a spokeswoman for the Centers for Medicare and Medicaid Services said the agency has given states no guidance on whether or how hospitals could be reimbursed for PTSD screenings. Hospitals are often unwilling to foot the bill themselves. Trauma surgeons and their staffs expressed frustration that they know PTSD is having a serious impact on their patients, but they can't find a way to pay for the help they need.

"We don't recognize that people have PTSD. We don't recognize that they're not doing their job as well, that they're not doing as well in school, that they're getting irritable at home with their families," said John Porter, a trauma surgeon in Jackson, Miss., which has a per capita homicide rate higher than Chicago's.

"If someone gets shot, and I save their life, and they can't go out and function—did I technically save their life? Probably not."

No One Gets Hardened

When RAND Corp. researchers began interviewing violently injured young men in Los Angeles in the late 1990s, they faced some skepticism that the men, often connected to gangs, would be susceptible to PTSD.

"We had people tell us that we'd see a lot of people who were gang-bangers, and they wouldn't develop PTSD, because they were already hardened to that kind of life," said Grant Marshall, a behavioral scientist who studied patients at a Los Angeles trauma center. "We didn't find that to be the case at all. People in gangs were just as likely as anyone else to develop PTSD."

In fact, trauma appears to have a cumulative effect. Young men with violent injuries may be more likely to develop symptoms if they have been attacked before.

The Los Angeles study found that 27 percent of the men interviewed three months after they were injured had symptoms consistent with PTSD.

"Most people still think that all the people who get shot were doing something they didn't need to be doing," said Porter, the trauma surgeon from Jackson, Miss. "I'm not saying it's the racist thing, but everybody thinks it's a young black men's disease: They get shot, they're out selling drugs. We're not going to spend more time on them."

While post-traumatic stress often does not show up until several months after an injury, experts say many trauma centers are missing the chance to evaluate patients early for risk of PTSD and to use clinical follow-ups—when patients come back to have their physical wounds examined—to check if patients are developing symptoms.

Required Screening Needed

Doctors say hospitals are unlikely to make significant progress until the American College of Surgeons makes systematic PTSD screening a requirement for all top-level trauma centers.

An ACS requirement would be "a much better hammer to show the administration," said Michael Foreman, chief of trauma surgery at Baylor University Medical Center in Dallas. Baylor, one of the few trauma centers to have a full-time psychologist on staff, surveyed 200 patients and found that roughly a quarter experienced post-traumatic stress. But Foreman said the center would not systematically screen all its patients until the ACS mandates it. It's not clear when that will happen. The organization's recognition of PTSD screening as a recommended practice is a first step. Those new guidelines will be released in March 2014, according to Chris Cribari,

Medical Procedures and Civilian PTSD

Although, historically, much of the initial interest in traumatic stress reactions has come from the field of military psychology and psychiatry, most of the PTSD [post-traumatic stress disorder] cases seen by practitioners in routine mental health practice, and that comprise the caseloads of most forensic examiners, involve civilian instances of PTSD from a variety of sources.

Emergency medical care, lifesaving though it may be, often employs procedures for which the patient has little or no preparation. The emotional impact of a serious illness or injury may be compounded by these invasive, painful, and frightening medical procedures, such as occurs in emergency treatment for a heart attack, motor vehicle accident, or workplace injury. Intrusive recollection and avoidance of stimuli are frequently observed among hospitalized survivors of trauma, but tend to be time limited and self-remitting. However, medical conditions or procedures themselves may constitute possible traumatic stressors as they are often associated with sudden onset, feelings of helplessness, lack of control by the patient, and/or a perceived or actual threat to life.

Laurence Miller,
PTSD and Forensic Psychology:
Applications to Civil and Criminal Law.
New York: Springer, 2015.

who chairs the subcommittee that evaluates whether hospitals are meeting ACS standards. Cribari declined to say when PTSD screening might become a requirement. He said the timing will depend on what hurdles hospitals encounter—such as patient privacy—when some of them start screenings.

Cribari acknowledged that at some hospitals, "unless it's a regulation, they're not going to spend the money on it."

At minimum, experts say, hospitals should provide all trauma patients with basic education about post-traumatic stress.

"The number one thing we do," is simply "tell everybody in the trauma center about PTSD," said John Nanney, a Department of Veterans Affairs researcher who developed a program for violently injured patients at the Spirit of Charity in New Orleans.

Without education about symptoms, patients who have flashbacks or constant nightmares may have "these catastrophic beliefs" about what is happening to them, Nanney said. "Just say, 'This is something you might notice. If you do notice it, it doesn't mean you're going crazy. It doesn't mean you're weak. This is something that happens—don't freak out.'"

The city of Philadelphia has begun to focus on trauma as a major public health issue. Philadelphia is working with local mental health providers to screen for PTSD more systematically—and to focus on post-traumatic stress as part of drug and alcohol treatment. The city has also paid to train local therapists in prolonged exposure, a proven treatment for PTSD—the same kind of training the U.S. Department of Veterans Affairs has paid for its therapists to receive.

For violently injured Philadelphia residents, there's also Drexel University's Healing Hurt People, a program that's become a national model for addressing trauma and PTSD.

Healing Hurt People reaches out to violently injured adults and children at two local hospitals and offers them intensive services. The program accepts a broad range of patients—from high schoolers to siblings of young men who have been shot to former drug dealers. (One of Healing Hurt People's clients talked about his post-traumatic stress in 2013 on *This American Life*.) The program's social workers screen all clients for PTSD symptoms and host discussions in which clients can share their experiences with one another. It's a way of fighting stigma around mental health symptoms. Instead of thinking that they're going crazy, the conversations help them realize, "OK, this is normal," as one client put it.

One of the program's central goals is to discourage victims of crimes from retaliating against their attackers and to help them focus on staying safe and rebuilding their own lives.

Understanding the Aftereffects of Trauma

The program's therapists and social workers remind clients that the aftereffects of trauma may make them overreact and help them plan how to identify and avoid events that might trigger them. In one discussion last fall, a therapist sketched a cliff on a whiteboard, with a stick man on the top, close to the edge. The question: How do you recognize when you're getting close to the cliff edge—and learn to walk away?

"Our thing is education," social worker Tony Thompson said. The more clients "understand what's going on in their body and their mind, the more prepared they are to deal with it."

Intensive casework like this has shown good results, but it's not cheap. Healing Hurt People is relatively small: Its programs served 129 new clients in 2013 and offered briefer education or assistance to a few hundred more. Its annual budget in 2013 was roughly $300,000, not including the cost of the office space that Drexel donates to the program.

Other researchers have been working to develop quicker, more modest interventions for PTSD, including some that use laptops and smartphones—programs that could easily be extended to more patients and still have some positive effect.

Whatever the approach, there "is untapped potential," said Joseph, the surgeon at Chicago's Cook County hospital. Healing Hurt People is a model for what she wants to create. "These are kids, for the most part. When a 17-year-old kid crashes their parents' car, and they were drinking, we don't say, 'Oh, that kid's hopeless, let's just give up on them.'"

"We've certainly had decades of trying to apply political solutions and social solutions to our inner cities' financial problems and violence problem, and they haven't been successful," said Ressler, the Atlanta researcher. "If we could do a better job of identification, intervention and treatment, I think there would be less violence, and people would have an easier time doing well in school, getting a job."

> *"The diagnostic criteria for PTSD ...*
> *represent a faulty, outdated construct*
> *that has been badly overextended so*
> *that it routinely mistakes depression,*
> *anxiety, or even normal adjustment for*
> *a unique and particularly stubborn ail-*
> *ment."*

The PTSD Trap: Our Overdiagnosis of PTSD in Vets Is Enough to Make You Sick

David Dobbs

David Dobbs writes on topics such as culture, science, and medi-cine for the New York Times, National Geographic, *and other publications. In the following viewpoint, he argues that post-traumatic stress disorder (PTSD) is greatly overdiagnosed. In part, this is because PTSD overlaps with other diagnoses, such as head trauma and depression. Also, Dobbs says, it is because health incentives in the United States encourage veterans to get a diagnosis of PTSD or lose health care. However, he argues, over-*

diagnosis of PTSD results in subpar treatment, strained resources, and poor outcomes. Dobbs concludes the diagnosis should be scaled back to provide better care to veterans.

As you read, consider the following questions:

1. How did the National Vietnam Veterans' Readjustment Study overstate PTSD, according to Dobbs?

2. How does Dobbs believe that false memories can confuse PTSD diagnosis?

3. How does the Australian system do a better job in handling PTSD, in Dobbs's view?

Author's note: This story originally appeared in *Scientific American*, April 2009. At the suggestion of medical student Petulant Skeptic (see below), I am republishing it . . . because the return of veterans of the Iraq and Afghanistan wars renews the importance of examining our ideas about how most soldiers react to combat. As noted in Petulant Skeptic's preface below, the U.S. press and populace seems all too ready to attribute every trouble suffered or made by combat veterans a sign of searing trauma. We can do better.—David Dobbs

Preface by Petulant Skeptic, U.S. Army

As America rushes to understand SSgt Robert Bales's alleged murder of 16 Afghan civilians [in Kandahar, Afghanistan, in 2012] there will be, and already is, a renewed interest in post-traumatic stress disorder (PTSD) and traumatic brain injury (TBI) among those who have served in Afghanistan and Iraq. While the media have been more restrained in blaming Bales's purported PTSD or TBI than they were with Benjamin Barnes—the Mt. Rainier shooter three months ago—there continues to be precious little examination of PTSD's prevalence and persistence among veterans. As a soldier, a medical student, and someone interested in these "invisible" injuries of war, I find myself often paraphrasing David's article in order to elucidate the confusing nomenclatures, conflated diagnoses and backwards incentives of how the Department of Veterans Affairs handles PTSD. Rather than rush to understand Bales, let's use this time to let the facts of *that* case settle and resolve—and take this as an opportunity to reexamine a broken system for the good of those who suffer below the radar of national calamity.

The Post-Traumatic Stress Trap

In 2006, soon after returning from military service in Ramadi, Iraq, during the bloodiest period of the war, Captain Matt Stevens of the Vermont National Guard began to have a problem with PTSD, or post-traumatic stress disorder. Stevens's problem was not that he had PTSD. It was that he began to have doubts about PTSD: The condition was real, he knew, but as a diagnosis he saw it being dangerously overemphasized.

Stevens led the medics tending an armored brigade of 800 soldiers, and his team patched together GIs and Iraqi citizens almost every day. He saw horrific things. Once home, he had his share, he says, of "nights where I'd wake up and it would be clear I wasn't going to sleep again."

He was not surprised: "I would *expect* people to have nightmares for a while when they came back." But as he kept track of his unit in the U.S., he saw troops greeted by both a larger culture and a medical culture, especially in the Department of Veterans Affairs (VA), that seemed reflexively to view bad memories, nightmares and any other sign of distress as an indicator of PTSD.

"Clinicians aren't separating the few who really have PTSD from those who are experiencing things like depression or anxiety or social reintegration problems, or who are just taking some time getting over it," says Stevens. He worries that many of these men and women are being pulled into a treatment and disability regime that will mire them in a self-fulfilling vision of a brain rewired, a psyche permanently haunted.

Stevens, now a major, and still on reserve duty while he works as a physician's assistant, is far from alone in worrying about the reach of PTSD. Over the last five years or so, a long-simmering academic debate over PTSD's conceptual basis and rate of occurrence has begun to boil over into the practice of trauma psychology and to roil military culture as well. Critiques, originally raised by military historians and a few psychologists, are now being advanced by a broad array of experts, including giants of psychology, psychiatry, diagnosis, and epidemiology such as Columbia's Robert Spitzer and Michael First, who oversaw the last two editions of the American Psychiatric Association's *Diagnostic and Statistical Manual of Mental Disorders*, the *DSM-III* and *DSM-IV*; Paul McHugh, the longtime chair of Johns Hopkins University's psychiatry department; Michigan State University epidemiologist Naomi Breslau; and Harvard University psychologist Richard Mc-Nally, a leading authority in the dynamics of memory and trauma, and perhaps the most forceful of the critics. The diagnostic criteria for PTSD, they assert, represent a faulty, outdated construct that has been badly overextended so that it routinely mistakes depression, anxiety, or even normal adjustment for a unique and particularly stubborn ailment.

This quest to scale back the definition of PTSD and its application stands to affect the expenditure of billions of dollars, the diagnostic framework of psychiatry, the effectiveness of a huge treatment and disability infrastructure, and, most important, the mental health and future lives of hundreds of thousands of U.S. combat veterans and other PTSD patients. Standing in the way of reform is conventional wisdom, deep cultural resistance and foundational concepts of trauma psychology. Nevertheless it is time, as Spitzer recently argued, to "save PTSD from itself."

Casting a Wide Net

The overdiagnosis of PTSD, critics say, shows in the numbers, starting with the seminal study of PTSD prevalence, the 1990 National Vietnam Veterans' Readjustment Study [NVVRS]. The NVVRS covered more than 1,000 Vietnam veterans in 1988 and reported that 15.4 percent of them had PTSD at that time and 31 percent had suffered it at some point since the war. That 31 percent has been the standard estimate of PTSD incidence among veterans ever since.

In 2006, however, Columbia University epidemiologist Bruce Dohrenwend, hoping to resolve nagging questions about the study, reworked the numbers. When he had culled the poorly documented diagnoses, he found that the 1988 rate was 9 percent, and the lifetime rate just 18 percent.

McNally shares the general admiration for Dohrenwend's careful work. Soon after it was published, however, McNally asserted that Dohrenwend's numbers were still too high because he counted as PTSD cases those veterans with only mild, subdiagnostic symptoms, people rated as "generally functioning pretty well." If you included only suffering "clinically significant impairment"—the level generally required for diagnosis and insurance compensation in most mental illness— the rates fell yet further, to 5.4 percent at the time of the survey and 11 percent for lifetime. It was not 1 in 3 veterans that eventually got PTSD, but 1 in 9—and only 1 in 18 had it at any given time. The NVVRS, in other words, appears to have overstated PTSD rates in Vietnam vets by almost 300 percent.

"PTSD is a real thing, without a doubt," says McNally. "But as a diagnosis, PTSD has become so flabby and overstretched, so much a part of the culture, that we are almost certainly mistaking other problems for PTSD, and thus mistreating them."

The idea that PTSD is overdiagnosed seems to contradict reports of resistance in the military and the VA to recognizing PTSD—denials of PTSD diagnoses and disability benefits, military clinicians discharging soldiers instead of treating them, and a disturbing increase in suicides among veterans of the Middle East wars. Yet the two trends are consistent. The VA's PTSD caseload has more than doubled since 2000, mostly owing to newly diagnosed Vietnam veterans. The poor and erratic response to current soldiers and recent vets, with some being pulled in quickly to PTSD treatments and others discouraged or denied, may be the panicked stumbling of an overloaded system.

Overhauling both the diagnosis and the VA's care system, say critics, will ensure better care for genuine PTSD patients as well as those being misdiagnosed. But the would-be reformers face fierce opposition. "This argument," McNally notes, "tends to really piss some people off." Veterans send him threatening emails. Colleagues accuse him of dishonoring veterans, dismissing suffering, discounting the costs of war. Dean Kilpatrick, a University of South Carolina traumatologist who is president of the International Society for Traumatic Stress Studies (ISTSS), once essentially called McNally a liar.

A Problematic Diagnosis

The most recent *Diagnostic and Statistical Manual (DSM-IV)* defines PTSD as the presence of three symptom clusters—reexperiencing via nightmares or flashbacks; numbing or withdrawal; and hyperarousal, evident in irritability, insomnia, aggression, or poor concentration—that arise in response to a life-threatening event.

Both halves of this definition are suspect. To start with, the link to a traumatic event, which makes PTSD almost unique among complex psychiatric diagnoses in being defined by an external cause, also makes it uniquely problematic, for the tie is really to the memory of an event. When PTSD was first added to the *DSM-III* in 1980, traumatic memories were considered reasonably faithful recordings of actual events. But as research since then has repeatedly shown, memory is spectacularly unreliable and extraordinarily malleable. We routinely add or subtract people, details, settings, and actions to our memories. We conflate, invent, and edit.

In one study by Washington University memory researcher Elizabeth Loftus, one out of four adults who were told they were lost in a shopping mall as children came to believe it. Some insisted the event happened even after the ruse was exposed. Bounteous research since then has confirmed that such false memories are common. (*See,* "Creating False Memories" by Elizabeth Loftus, *Scientific American*, Sept. 1997.)

Soldiers enjoy no immunity from this tendency. A 1990s study at the New Haven, Connecticut, VA hospital asked 59 Gulf War veterans about their war experiences a month after their return and again two years later. The researchers asked about 19 specific types of potentially traumatic events, such as witnessing deaths, losing friends, and seeing people disfigured. Two years out, 70 percent of the veterans reported at least one traumatic event they had not mentioned a month after returning, and 24 percent reported at least three such events for the first time. And the veterans recounting the most "new memories" also reported the most PTSD symptoms.

To McNally, such results suggest that some veterans experiencing "late-onset" PTSD may be attributing symptoms of depression, anxiety, or other subtle disorders to a memory that has been elaborated and given new significance—or even unconsciously (and innocently) fabricated.

"This has nothing to do with gaming or working the system or consciously looking for sympathy," he says. "We all do this: We cast our lives in terms of narratives that help us understand them. A vet who's having a difficult life may remember a trauma, which may or may not have actually traumatized him, and everything makes sense." To make PTSD diagnosis more rigorous, some have suggested that blood chemistry, brain imaging or other tests might be able to detect physiological signatures of PTSD. Studies of stress hormones in groups of PTSD patients show differences from normal subjects, but the overlap between the normal and the PTSD groups is huge, making individual profiles useless for diagnostics. Brain imaging has similar limitations, with the abnormal dynamics in PTSD heavily overlapping those of depression and anxiety.

With memory unreliable and biological markers elusive, diagnosis depends on clinical symptoms. But as a 2007 study showed starkly, PTSD's symptom profile is as slippery as the would-be biomarkers. J. Alexander Bodkin, a psychiatrist at Harvard's McLean Hospital, screened 90 clinically depressed patients separately for PTSD symptoms and for trauma, then compared the results. First he and a colleague used a standardized PTSD screening interview to assess PTSD symptoms. Then two other PTSD diagnosticians, ignorant of the symptom reports, used a standard interview to see which patients had ever experienced trauma fitting *DSM-IV* criteria.

If PTSD arose from trauma, the patients with PTSD symptoms should have histories of trauma, and those with trauma should show more PTSD. It was not so. While the symptom screens rated 70 of the 90 patients PTSD-positive, the trauma screens found only 54 who had suffered trauma; the diagnosed PTSD "cases" outnumbered those who had experienced traumatic events. Things got worse when Bodkin compared the diagnoses one-on-one. If PTSD required trauma, then the 54 trauma-exposed patients should account for most of the 70 PTSD-positive patients. But the PTSD-symptomatic patients were equally distributed among the trauma-positive and the trauma-negative groups. The PTSD rate had zero relation to the trauma rate. It was, Bodkin observed, "a scientifically unacceptable situation."

More practically, as McNally points out, "To give the best treatment, you have to have the right diagnosis."

The most effective treatment for patients whose symptoms arose from trauma is exposure-based cognitive behavioral therapy (CBT), which concentrates on altering the response to a specific traumatic memory by repeated, controlled exposure to it. "And it works," says McNally. "If someone with genuine PTSD goes to the people who do this really well, they have a good chance of getting better." CBT for depression, in contrast, teaches the patient to recognize dysfunctional loops of thought and emotion and develop new responses to normal, present-day events. "If a depressed person takes on a PTSD interpretation of their troubles and gets exposure-based CBT, you're going to miss the boat," says McNally. "You're going to spend your time chasing this memory down instead of dealing with the way the patient misinterprets present events."

To complicate the matter, recent studies show that traumatic brain injuries from bomb blasts, common among soldiers in Iraq, produce symptoms almost indistinguishable from PTSD. One more overlapping symptom set.

"The overlap issue worries me tremendously," says Gerald Rosen, a University of Washington psychiatrist who has worked extensively with PTSD patients. "We have to ask how we got here. We have to ask ourselves, 'What do *we* gain by having this diagnosis?'"

Disabling Conditions

Rosen is thinking of clinicians when he asks about gain. But what does a veteran gain with a PTSD diagnosis? One would hope, of course, that it grants access to effective treatment and support. This is not happening. In civilian populations, two-thirds of PTSD patients respond to treatment. But as psychologist Chris Frueh, who researched and treated PTSD for the VA from the early 1990s until 2006, notes, "In the two largest VA studies of combat veterans, neither showed a treatment effect. Vets getting PTSD treatment from the VA are no more likely to get better than they would on their own."

The reason, says Frueh, is the collision of the PTSD construct's vagaries with the VA's disability system, in which every benefit seems structured to discourage recovery.

The first benefit is health care. PTSD is by far the easiest mental health diagnosis to have declared "service-connected," a designation that often means the difference between little or no care and broad, lasting health coverage. Service connection also makes a vet eligible for monthly disability payments of up to $4,000. That link may explain why most veterans getting PTSD treatment from the VA report worsening symptoms until they are designated 100 percent disabled—at which point their use of VA mental health services drops by 82 percent. It may also help to explain why, although the risk of PTSD from a traumatic event drops as time passes, the number of Vietnam veterans applying for PTSD disability almost doubled between 1999 and 2004, driving total PTSD disability payments to more than $4 billion annually. Perhaps most disastrously, these payments continue only if you're sick. For unlike a vet who has lost a leg, a vet with PTSD loses disability benefits as soon as he recovers or starts working. The entire system seems designed to encourage chronic disability.

"In the several years I spent in VA PTSD clinics," says Frueh, "I can't think of a single PTSD patient who left treatment because he got better. But the problem is not the veterans. The problem is that the VA's disability system, which is 60 years old now, ignores all the intervening research we have on resilience, on the power of expectancy and the effects of incentives and disincentives. Sometimes I think they should just blow it up and start over." But with what?

Richard Bryant, an Australian PTSD researcher and clinician, suggests a disability system more like that Down Under. An Australian soldier injured in combat receives a lifelong "noneconomic" disability payment of $300 to $1,200 monthly. If the injury keeps her from working, she also gets an "incapacity" payment, as well as job training and help finding work.

Finally—a crucial feature—she retains all these benefits for two years once she goes back to work. After that, her incapacity payments taper to zero over five years. But her noneconomic payments—a sort of financial Purple Heart—continue forever. And like all Australians, she gets free lifetime health care. Australian vets come home to an utterly different support system from ours: Theirs is a scaffold they can climb. Ours is a low-hanging "safety net" liable to trap anyone who falls in.

Two Ways to Carry a Rifle

When a soldier comes home, he must try to reconcile his war experience with the person he was beforehand and the society and family he returns to. He must engage in what psychologist Rachel Yehuda, who researches PTSD at the Bronx VA hospital, calls "recontextualization"—the process of integrating trauma into normal experience. It is what we all do, on a smaller scale, when we suffer breakups, job losses, the deaths of loved ones. Initially the event seems an impossible aberration. Then slowly we accept the trauma as part of the complex context that is life.

Matt Stevens recognizes this can take time. Even after a year home, the war still occupies his dreams. Sometimes, for instance, he dreams that he is doing something completely normal—while carrying his combat rifle.

"One night I dreamt I was birdwatching with my wife. When we saw a bird, she would lift her binoculars, and I would lift my rifle and watch the bird through the scope. No thought of shooting it. Just how I looked at the birds." It would be easy to read Stevens's dream as a symptom of PTSD, expressing fear, hypervigilance, and avoidance. Yet, the dream can also be seen as demonstrating his success in recontextualizing his experience. He is reconciling the man who once used a gun with the man who no longer does.

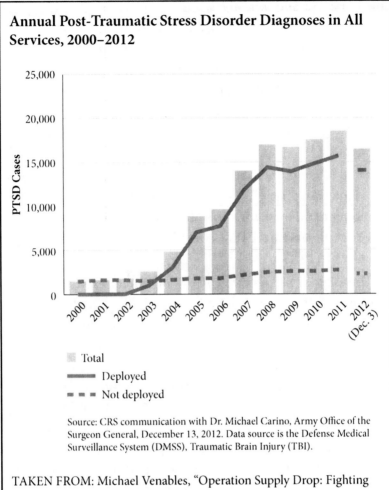

Annual Post-Traumatic Stress Disorder Diagnoses in All Services, 2000–2012

Total

Deployed

Not deployed

Source: CRS communication with Dr. Michael Carino, Army Office of the Surgeon General, December 13, 2012. Data source is the Defense Medical Surveillance System (DMSS), Traumatic Brain Injury (TBI).

TAKEN FROM: Michael Venables, "Operation Supply Drop: Fighting PTSD and Bolstering Troop Morale, One Video Game Care Package at a Time," *Forbes*, March 1, 2013.

Saving PTSD from itself, say Spitzer, McNally, Frueh, and other critics, will require a similar shift—seeing most post-combat distress not as a disorder but as part of normal, if painful, healing. This will involve, for starters, revising the PTSD diagnosis construct—presently under review for the new *DSM-5* due to be published in 2012—so it accounts for the unreliability of memory and better distinguishes depression, anxiety, and phobia from true PTSD. Mental health evaluations need similar revisions so they can detect genuine cases without leading patients to impose trauma narratives on other mental health problems. Finally, Congress should replace the VA's disability regime with an evidence-based system that removes disincentives to recovery—and even go the extra mile and give all combat veterans, injured or not, lifetime health care.

These changes will be hard to sell in a culture that resists any suggestion that PTSD is not a common, even inevitable, consequence of combat. Mistaking its horror for its prevalence, people assume PTSD is epidemic, ignoring all evidence to the contrary.

The biggest longitudinal study of soldiers returning from Iraq and Afghanistan, led by VA researcher Charles Milliken and published in 2007, seemed to confirm that we should expect a high incidence of PTSD. It surveyed combat troops immediately on return from deployment and again 6 months later and found around 20 percent symptomatically "at risk" of PTSD. But of those reporting symptoms in the first survey, half had improved by the second survey, and many who first claimed few or no symptoms later reported serious symptoms. How many of the early "symptoms" were just normal adjustment? How many of the later symptoms were the imposition of a trauma narrative onto other problems? Matt Stevens, for one, is certain these screens are mistaking many going through normal adjustment as dangerously at risk of PTSD. Even he, although functioning fine at work, home, and in society, scored positive in *both* surveys; he is, in other words, one of the 20 percent "at risk." Finally, and weirdly, both screens missed about 75 percent of those who actually sought counseling—a finding that raises further doubts about the screens' accuracy. Yet this study received prominent media coverage emphasizing that PTSD rates were probably being badly undercounted.

A few months later, another study—the first to track large numbers of soldiers through the war—provided a clearer and more consistent picture. Led by U.S. Navy researcher Tyler Smith and published in the *British Medical Journal*, the study monitored mental health and combat exposure in 50,000 U.S. soldiers from 2001 to 2006. The researchers took particular care to tie symptoms to types of combat exposure and demographic factors. Among the 20,000 troops who went to Iraq, 4.3 percent developed diagnosis-level symptoms of PTSD. The rate ran about 8 percent in those with combat exposure and 2 percent in those not exposed.

These numbers are about a quarter of the rates Milliken found. But they're a close match of PTSD rates seen in British Iraq War vets and to rates McNally calculated for Vietnam veterans. The contrast to the Milliken study, along with the consistency with British rates and with McNally's NVVRS calculation, should have made the Smith study big news. Yet the media, the VA, and the trauma psychology community almost completely ignored the study. "The silence," McNally wryly noted, "was deafening."

This silence may be merely a matter of good news going unremarked. Yet it supports McNally's contention that we have a cultural obsession with trauma. The selective attention supports too the assertion by military historian and PTSD critic Ben Shephard that American society itself gained something from the creation of the PTSD diagnosis in the late 1970s: a vision of war's costs that transforms our soldiers from perpetrators to victims—and in doing so, absolves the rest of us for sending them, for we too were victimized, fooled into supporting a war we later regretted. It's good that we feel soldiers' pain. But to impose on a distressed soldier the notion that his memories are inescapable, that he lacks the strength to incorporate his past into his future, is to highlight our moral sensitivity at the soldier's expense.

PTSD exists. Where it exists, we must treat it. But our cultural obsession with PTSD has magnified and replicated and institutionalized PTSD until it has finally become the thing itself—a prolonged failure to contextualize and accept our own collective aggression. It may be our own postwar neurosis.

> *"The epidemic of male suicide has been silent, but it cannot remain so. Only by breaking the silence . . . will we overcome this epidemic."*

Raising Public Awareness May Reduce Male Suicide

Dan Bilsker and Jennifer White

Dan Bilsker is a health services researcher with the Centre for Applied Research in Mental Health and Addiction at Simon Fraser University and a clinical assistant professor in the Faculty of Medicine at the University of British Columbia. Jennifer White is an assistant professor in the School of Child and Youth Care at the University of Victoria. In the following viewpoint, they argue that male suicide rates are high compared with such rates for women. The danger of male suicide specifically has largely been ignored because of a lack of public awareness and because of men's reluctance to discuss depression or suicidal thoughts. The authors conclude that the silence surrounding male suicide must be broken if the problem is to be addressed.

Dan Bilsker and Jennifer White, "The Silent Epidemic of Male Suicide," *BC Medical Journal*, vol. 53, no. 10, December 2011. Copyright © 2011 BC Medical Journal. All rights reserved. Reproduced with permission.

As you read, consider the following questions:

1. Why do the authors say that suicide as an epidemic is "silent"?

2. According to Bilsker and White, what differences are there in suicide attempts between men and women?

3. According to the viewpoint, what are some possible explanations for the differences between men and women who reach the point of suicidal action?

A lack of public awareness and too few explanatory frameworks and preventive efforts specifically targeting male suicide have made a major public health problem largely invisible.

A Silent Epidemic

Suicide in men has been described as a "silent epidemic": epidemic because of its high incidence and substantial contribution to men's mortality, and silent because of a lack of public awareness, a paucity of explanatory research, and the reluctance of men to seek help for suicide-related concerns. A statistical overview demonstrates a shockingly high rate of death by suicide for men compared with women, and a need to focus attention on prevention, screening, treatment, and service delivery. Promising lines of research include identification of clinical indicators specifically predictive of male suicide and exploration of precipitating and predisposing factors that distinguish male suicide and account for the substantial gender disparity. Only by breaking the silence—building public awareness, refining explanatory frameworks, implementing preventive strategies, and undertaking research—will we overcome this epidemic.

Suicide in men has been described as a "silent epidemic." It has a disturbingly high incidence and is a major contributor to men's mortality. In British Columbia [BC], suicide is one of the top three causes of mortality among men aged 15 and 44. Among men of all ages in Canada, suicide ranked as the seventh leading cause of death in 2007.

The silence surrounding suicide among men is also striking and warrants comment. First, there appears to be an overall lack of public awareness regarding the high rates of suicide among men, especially relative to other more highly publicized threats to men's health, such as HIV/AIDS, that account for far fewer premature deaths among males each year (e.g., in 2005, 45 male deaths were attributed to AIDS in Canada in contrast to 2857 male deaths from suicide).

Second, while accumulating empirical evidence confirms that men in Western nations consistently die by suicide at higher rates than women (with the pattern reversed for nonfatal suicidal behaviors), surprisingly few explanatory frameworks have been developed to account for this persistent pattern.

Third, few preventive efforts or policies specifically targeting male suicide have been developed or evaluated, which further contributes to its lack of visibility as a major public health problem. When gender is addressed it is often treated as a static demographic variable as opposed to a culturally mediated social construction that intersects with other diversity markers such as race, sexual orientation, and age in highly complex ways.

Finally, given men's general reluctance to seek help for suicide-related concerns, and the stigma associated with mental health problems in general, it is no surprise that suicide among men is largely invisible.

A statistical overview of the magnitude of the problem within a Canadian context reveals that suicide claims the lives of nearly 3000 men each year. Findings from a range of intellectual traditions and disciplines, including contributions from quantitative and qualitative research paradigms, reveal much about the consequences of male suicide to society. These consequences lead in turn to discussion of prevention, screening, treatment, and service delivery issues, as well as recommendations for future research.

Magnitude of the Problem

Men have a shockingly high rate of death by suicide compared with women. Across all countries reporting these data (except China and India) males show a suicide rate that is 3.0 to 7.5 times that of women. In Canada, the male suicide rate is about three times that of women. [The graph in this viewpoint] charts the age- and gender-specific incidence of suicide in Canada, based on data from 2001 to 2005. Two patterns are worth noting:

- The male suicide rate increases fairly steadily with age, peaking in the late 40s, then falling significantly and rising again in the 80s.

- Male rates are greater than female rates at all ages and substantially greater across most of the life span.

The male pattern showing a peak in suicide rate among Canadian men in their 40s and 50s is surprising in light of multinational data showing one of two patterns: a steady increase in suicide rate with age or a peak of suicide in younger age groups. However, a change in this suicide pattern may be under way, at least in North America.

Among US white men, middle age has historically been a time of relatively lower risk of completed suicide, compared with elderly men. Yet by 2005, the suicide rate of white men aged 45 to 49 years was not only higher than the rate for men aged less than 40 years but also slightly higher than the rate for men aged 70 to 74 years ... suicide-prevention efforts have focused most heavily on the groups considered to be most at risk: teens and young adults of both genders as well as elderly white men. ... Suicide in the middle-adult years has not been studied as extensively.

It is apparent that our knowledge of men's suicide is lagging behind changes in the age-specific incidence of this cause of death. Until we understand the underlying reasons for this relative increase in men's suicide rates in middle age, including potential cohort effects, we will not be able to implement effective preventive action.

While the analysis of suicide rates is highly informative, some epidemiologists have argued that a more useful way to evaluate suicide impact is in terms of potential years of life lost (PYLL), which reflects both mortality rate and age at which death occurs.

"This measure takes into account an argument that the death of a young person involves more loss than that of an older person. This alternative measure incorporates the notion that one death is not implicitly the same as another death. This notion is particularly important when one seeks to weigh the importance of suicide relative to other causes of death."

Suicide is the second leading cause of potential years of life lost by men compared with women, reflecting both men's higher rate of suicide and the relatively young age at which many suicide deaths occur. In Canada, suicide accounts for about 10% of all PYLL for men; in BC, it accounts for about 7%.

We also need to look at suicide attempts to understand the gender difference in suicidal behavior. Although men die by suicide at a higher rate, women have a higher rate of attempting suicide. This pattern is evident among youth and persists over the life span. . . .

It should be noted that there is a spectrum of self-harm, ranging from acts of physical self-harm not intended to be suicidal, to acts that reflect ambivalence about dying, to acts that reflect a clear and settled intention to die. The broad term deliberate self-harm (DSH) is often used in the research literature to capture this range of possible actions. As one might expect from the suicide attempt statistics, women show much higher rates of DSH.

Prevention

We do not fully understand the complexity of suicide, including the reasons for the gender difference in suicidal behavior. This makes it particularly challenging to develop effective prevention programs that can address the high rates of suicide in men specifically.

What are the factors contributing to men's higher rate of death by suicide; and, in particular, why do such a high proportion of male suicide attempts end in death? As noted in a recent review of suicide risk screening, "dramatic differences in suicide behaviors among men and women ... have drawn little attention. A better understanding of these variations may have direct implications for screening and treatment strategies, and they warrant further research."

One line of investigation has focused on suicide methods. A well-established finding is that men are more likely to use suicide methods of high lethality, methods with increased risk of death. For example, a recent pan-European study found that the highly lethal methods of hanging and firearms were more likely to be used by men. Sixty-two percent of males, versus 40% of females, used hanging or firearms in their suicidal actions.

Other investigators have confirmed that compared with suicidal women who use firearms to shoot themselves in the body, men are more apt to shoot themselves in the head, increasing the likelihood of death.

These findings suggest that restricting access to firearms might be a way to achieve a relative reduction in male suicide, and there is some tentative support for this as an important suicide prevention strategy. In contrast, it is next to impossible to reduce access to ligatures and suspension points commonly used in hanging deaths since these materials are widely available in the community.

From another point of view, we could ask why men are more likely to choose methods of high lethality. With regard

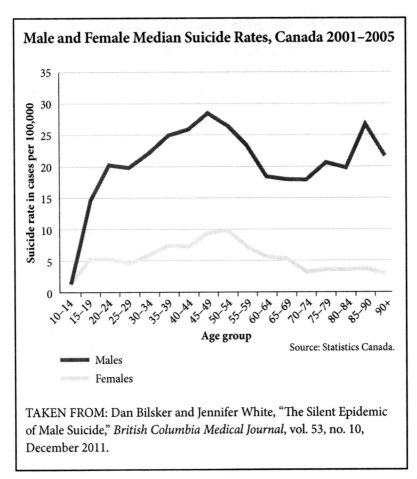

Male and Female Median Suicide Rates, Canada 2001–2005

Source: Statistics Canada.

Males
Females

TAKEN FROM: Dan Bilsker and Jennifer White, "The Silent Epidemic of Male Suicide," *British Columbia Medical Journal*, vol. 53, no. 10, December 2011.

to the use of firearms, it may be that men have more familiarity with and exposure to guns and thus are more likely to use this method. But when it comes to hanging, the picture is far more complex. For example, proportionally, women choose hanging as a method of suicide almost as frequently as men.

Here in British Columbia for example, hanging was the most common method of suicide for men and women in 2009, accounting for 48% and 38% of suicide deaths respectively. This observation undermines a simplistic, dichotomous understanding of the role of methods (i.e., more lethal versus less lethal) when attempting to account for the persistent gender gap in suicide.

Why Men Are More Successful at Suicide

Researchers have speculated about other reasons men may have for employing highly lethal means. These explanations suggest that when compared with suicidal women, men who reach the point of suicidal action are:

- More hopeless.

- More clearly resolved to die.

- More likely to be intoxicated and thus more disinhibited.

- More willing to carry out actions that might leave them injured or disfigured.

- More unconcerned with consequences because of a high risk-taking orientation.

- More likely to have a greater capacity to enact lethal self-injury.

Despite some limited theoretical and empirical support, we currently lack strong evidence to support these explanations.

A study of suicide attempts in older men and women showed that men were more intent upon dying and moved more quickly and decisively from considering suicide to acting upon the suicidal ideation. The study noted, "Our findings suggest that factors responsible for the increased suicide rate in older men operate largely during the suicidal crisis itself: once a depressed older man develops serious suicidal intent, he tends to realize it with little hesitation." The reasons men move in this unhesitating way to suicidal behavior remain to be determined.

Men's lack of social support, relative to that available to women, has been implicated as a risk factor in male suicide. An interview-based study of men who had attempted suicide suggested that social stressors—family breakdown, overwork, employment insecurity—often combined with alcohol or drug abuse, are understudied contributors to male suicide. Some evidence suggests that occupational stress contributes more strongly to male than female suicide.

Consistent with men's relatively low levels of help-seeking for psychological difficulties, a review of help-seeking by individuals who eventually died by suicide showed that men had lower overall rates of contact with the formal health care system (including primary care and mental health services) compared with women.

Specifically, in the year before suicide, an average 58% of women versus 35% of men sought care from a mental health practitioner. In contrast, an average 78% of men who died by suicide had contact with their primary care provider within the year prior to their suicide, lending support to the role played by primary care providers in suicide prevention.

Other promising approaches include community-wide interventions aimed at changing social norms. For example, in response to low help-seeking and rising suicide rates among men in the early 1990s, the US Air Force developed an innovative population-level suicide prevention strategy that was designed to change norms around help-seeking, improve community-wide awareness of suicide risks, and increase the use of local resources.

This systematic effort, which targeted the whole community, was associated with a sustained decline in suicide rates, providing some preliminary support for this multilevel, early intervention approach.

Screening and Risk Formulation

There are no special protocols or instruments recommended for screening men for suicidality in primary care. The typical recommended approach focuses on screening for depression (which is a common precursor of suicide) using brief questionnaires, which are typically the same for men and women.

One might expect that men's well-established reluctance to discuss relationship or emotional difficulties would call for more careful screening of men by health care providers, but there is not yet significant evidence supporting the effectiveness of a differential approach to men's depression or suicide risk.

Likewise, the evaluation of suicidality in men typically follows the same general protocol as that for women. At the same time, certain risk factors are more predictive of male suicide, suggesting we should pay greater attention to these factors when evaluating suicidality in men.

One study tracked individuals with the diagnosis of major depression over 2 years and found certain variables to be much more predictive of suicidal acts in men than in women: a family history of suicidal behavior, previous drug use, and early parental separation. Male suicides are more likely to occur in the context of substance use disorders than are female suicides.

Men also show much higher levels of alcohol abuse— given the pervasive effects associated with abuse of alcohol and other drugs, it is not surprising to find an associated increase in suicide. This should be a key component in the assessment of male suicidality. Protective factors are important to consider in any comprehensive suicide risk assessment, and evidence suggests that protective factors may differ for men and women. For example, being married appears to be a greater protective factor for men than for women.

Research Possibilities

To date, there has not been research to determine whether intervention for suicidality is comparably effective for men and women and whether suicidal men should be approached with different treatment modalities.

A recent review of gender differences in suicide recommended that "research on treatments for suicidal behavior should investigate gender differences in response. Initiatives to develop gender-specific approaches may be indicated. Gender differences in suicidal behavior clearly merit more research attention to generate information that can guide clinical practice and prevention strategies in ways that will prove most effective for preventing suicidal behavior in both genders."

It is remarkable how little we have learned about causal factors and preventive strategies specifically relevant to male suicide. One would think that the hugely elevated rate of suicide in men compared with women would have sparked a substantial investment of resources into systematic research and enhanced clinical practice. Instead, the high rate of male suicide has been treated as somehow natural and inevitable. The time has come to give this problem high priority.

One line of research might focus upon clinical indicators that are specifically predictive for male suicide. Recognition of suicide indicators in clinical practice is especially problematic, given the disinclination of male patients to talk about emotional distress and their greater propensity for impulsive behavior. The development and validation of protocols for male-appropriate suicide assessment and intervention would greatly support health care providers in responding effectively to men's suicide risk.

Another line of research would examine the precipitating and predisposing factors that distinguish male suicide and account for the substantial gender disparity in suicide mortality. Why do men use more lethal methods, why do they move with less hesitation from thinking about suicide to implementing it, and why are they more reluctant to seek help in dealing with the stressors that contribute to suicide?

A richer understanding of the pathways to suicide characteristic of men will give us a stronger basis for designing programs to prevent suicide in the general male population and the subpopulation of men with identified mental health problems.

The epidemic of male suicide has been silent, but it cannot remain so. Only by breaking the silence—building public awareness, refining explanatory frameworks, implementing preventive strategies, and undertaking research—will we overcome this epidemic.

"The uncomfortable truth is that stereo-typical forms of masculinity—stiff up-per lips, 'laddishness'—are killing men."

Addressing Stigma and Masculinity May Reduce Male Suicide

Owen Jones

Owen Jones is a columnist for the Guardian *and the author of* Chavs: The Demonization of the Working Class. *In the follow-ing viewpoint, he writes that in Britain, suicide is the main cause of death in men under fifty, and that men kill themselves at much higher rates than women. He argues that stereotypical male expectations of strength and competence prevent men from seeking help or discussing depression. Jones concludes that Brit-ain needs to invest more in mental health care and encourage more men to come forward to confront toxic male stereotypes.*

As you read, consider the following questions:

1. According to Jones, who is Jake Mills?

2. Why is the prevalence of gay insults linked to suicide, in Jones's view?

3. What evidence does Jones provide that men will not get the mental health funds they need from the government?

Nine months ago, Jake Mills texted his girlfriend one final time to tell her he loved her—and then he tried to kill himself. "I genuinely felt that I was a burden to a lot of people's lives," the 25-year-old Liverpool comedian says. "A lot of people say suicide is a selfish act but, in that frame of mind, if you're about to kill yourself, you just don't see anything better."

The Biggest Killer of Men

Although Jake had been visiting a counsellor, he was just telling her what he thought she wanted to hear. "She discharged me and told me that I was healthy and better. But actually I wasn't better, I was just better at lying."

Jake was rescued by his girlfriend and has been confronting his depression ever since. But for all too many men, there is no rescue. Last week [in August 2014], millions were shocked by the suicide of beloved actor Robin Williams. The aftermath has provoked a long-neglected debate about mental health and suicide.

A cursory look at the statistics in Britain suggests it is dearly needed. Suicide is the biggest killer of men between 20 and 49, eclipsing road accidents, cancer and coronary heart disease. It is also predominantly a male disorder. Of the 5,981 suicides in 2012, an astonishing 4,590 (76%) were men. And yet while Britain has high-profile campaigns on, say, testicular cancer or driving safely, the biggest killer of men under 50 is not getting the attention it deserves.

Jane Powell is the founder and director of Calm, the Campaign Against Living Miserably, which specifically deals with male suicide. "If you're a mum, a dad, a loved one, you want to worry about the biggest threat," she says. "And yet we worry about assault levels, rather than the real killer—suicide." She makes a provocative case: that while breast cancer does kill men, we rightly focus on it as a female disease. In the same way, suicide prevention has to focus on men. "We need to name the issue," she says.

Why are so many more men killing themselves than women? "Is it biologically set in stone that men take their own lives—or is it cultural?" Powell asks. "If you look at how the suicide rates have changed, how they go up and down, you can see that it's cultural—it's about what we expect." And this is what is so troubling about male suicide. Women are actually more likely to suffer from depression, but more likely to seek help when they encounter trouble. The uncomfortable truth is that stereotypical forms of masculinity—stiff upper lips, "laddishness"—are killing men.

Ant Meads, a 35-year-old based in Coventry, tried to end his life nearly two years ago. Growing up, he had undiagnosed obsessive-compulsive disorder (OCD). "I was 18, working in a concrete yard, surrounded by big burly men doing manual labour, and I was a stick insect," he recalls.

Whenever his hands were dirty, he felt nauseous, so he wore gloves all the time. "I got bullied every single day when I was there, I was the 'little special princess who has to have his special gloves'. It was the first time I realised that I was not living up to the ideal of what a man should be."

His OCD would get worse, until he was too anxious to leave the house. "I was failing myself, my family, society, because I couldn't do what every man was supposed to be able to do." He was left with a sense of worthlessness, of letting people down.

When he first told his father that he was depressed, he told him to "get over it". It wasn't just relatives: doctors told him to "get on with it" as well. When a doctor finally referred

him to psychiatric care, Meads faced a six-week wait before finally being seen by a community liaison officer, who disputed
whether he had OCD because—unlike other patients—his
hands were not chapped. "It's this horrible idea of what a man
is supposed to be," he explains. "It's a general feeling, evident
in the fact that so many men commit suicide, because they're
not living up to this mythical idea."

Uncomfortable with Feelings

This sense that men should not speak about their feelings is
not always overt; nor does it necessarily manifest itself as bullying. Fabio Zucchelli, 29, has had depression since his early
teenage years. "I noticed that I was low for very long periods,
and it developed into what people term clinical depression,"
he says. "It certainly held me back in many ways, up to my
early to mid-20s. . . . There have been long periods when I've
felt not able to work at all."

Zucchelli says he didn't suffer from "self-stigmatising issues", and has been able to talk about his feelings with professionals. "The main issue I've had with feeling able to talk
about mental health difficulties is with male friends, who just
find it really uncomfortable. I haven't had anyone defriend me
because of it, just a lot of discomfort."

When the 35-year-old Labour MP [member of Parlia-
ment] John Woodcock announced last December that he was
depressed, he was confronting a double stigma: not just as a
man talking about his mental health, but as a politician discussing a personal issue that is all too often portrayed as a
weakness.

"I've been really struck by the number of men who have
come up to me—often in my constituency—like ex-shipyard
workers who have struggled for 10 years, who have been keeping it quiet," he tells me. "We do operate in a culture where
men, by and large, talk about their feelings less. They're self-

conscious about talking about weakness, there's this male sense of 'shrug and get on with stuff'."

This type of male identity is cemented at a very young age. According to research by the LGB [lesbian, gay, bisexual] charity Stonewall, 98% of gay pupils and 95% of teachers hear "that's so gay" or "you're so gay" at school; nearly as many hear "dyke" or "poof" thrown around as insults. "It's so much wider than gay or bisexual men," says Stonewall's spokesman Richard Lane. "Men hear 'man up' and 'stop being such a poof'. It's a real barrier in talking about mental health issues."

Gender Policing

Rather than being entirely about anti-gay hatred, there is an element of "gender policing", of abuse directed at men who do not conform to a stereotype of masculinity.

"Asking for help is seen as an affront to masculinity," says the writer Laurie Penny, who has extensively researched mental health issues and written about her own experiences. "This is deeply, deeply troubling, because it means when you're taking that first step when you're suffering a mental health difficulty, reaching out for help is made doubly hard. The rules of masculinity prevent you from asking for help or talking about feelings."

According to Penny, depression is often accompanied by a sense of shame, of not deserving help, "and when messed-up gender roles are thrown into the mix, it's going to become even more troubling". She has no doubt that gender policing "ruins lives across the board".

Mind is one of Britain's main mental health charities; according to its research, just 23% of men would see a GP [general practitioner] if they felt low for more than two weeks, compared with 33% of women. "One of the more common ways men deal with it is self-medicating with alcohol and drugs," says the Mind spokeswoman Beth Murphy. "They start going to the pub, block feelings, hide feelings, drink, then do it more, and it becomes a cycle. The drugs and alcohol can end up as big a problem as the mental distress in the first place." Indeed, research has suggested that men are twice as likely as women to develop alcoholism.

In the late 1990s, it was men in their 20s who were most at risk from suicide; today it is men in their 40s. As Murphy points out, it's the same cohort, and is evidence of "scarring": of being unemployed at a young age, and suffering from long-term consequences, including higher rates of unemployment and lower wages in later life, as well as mental distress.

According to research by Samaritans, those in the poorest socioeconomic circumstances are 10 times more likely to kill themselves than those in the most affluent. Both men and women experience poverty, of course—but it is men who are more likely to kill themselves if they are poor.

And the help simply is not there for men, even if they seek it. When Ant Meads finally saw the doctor who instantly recognised his OCD and began a referral for specialist care, he faced a nine-month wait. "Imagine you're suicidal, you need to see a psychiatrist, and you're told the current waiting list is nine months. How do people cope?" Meads is adamant that he would not be alive had his employer not referred him to private health care. He believes there needs to be far more government investment and a national advertising blitz about men and mental health.

But the winds are blowing against Meads's calls: mental health trusts are making cuts amounting to 20% more than those made by other hospitals; mental health services have cut beds by nearly 10% in the past three years, and mental health organisations have warned that cuts to such services are risking people's lives.

"I'm really concerned about it," says Woodcock. "We've now made the commitment that mental health should have parity with physical conditions in the NHS [National Health Service], but we're not close to delivering that parity."

Unless this changes, he suggests, "we'll fail many people who will suffer mental health conditions, or even suicide, when they can be helped."

Challenging unreconstructed masculinity is surely a priority, too. The organisation Calm has launched an initiative called "#mandictionary", encouraging men to take on "archaic male stereotypes" and "define themselves on their own terms". Men speaking out—as they have done in this [viewpoint]—helps, too, encouraging others to come forward. "From a personal point of view, I'd never admit to anyone I was depressed, I didn't even want to be on antidepressants because of the stigma attached," Jake Mills explains.

"I thought I'd be addicted to them and weak." Now he uses his comedy to raise the issue. "The best decision I made in my life was announcing it, going on Twitter. I've had enough, I'm not hiding from it anymore."

Speaking out and challenging the stigma of mental health is certainly courageous. And doing so may just help to save the lives of other men who are suffering in agonising, lonely silence.

Periodical and Internet Sources Bibliography

The following articles have been selected to supplement the diverse views presented in this chapter.

Jesse Barron — "The Journalist and the Suicide," *New Inquiry*, July 21, 2014.

Evie Blad — "Sandy Hook Shooter's Needs Went Unmet by Schools," *Education Week*, December 3, 2014.

Cathryn Domrose — "A Few Good Women: U.S. Female Veterans with PTSD Are Getting Better Care," Nurse.com, February 9, 2015.

Rebecca Falconer — "Britain in Male Suicide Crisis—Because Real Men Don't Suffer Depression," *International Business Times*, February 19, 2015.

James Gallagher — "Suicide in Men 'Highest Since 2001,'" BBC, February 19, 2015.

Robert David Jaffee — "Men, Mental Illness and Suicide," *Huffington Post*, September 20, 2013.

Sebastian Junger — "How PTSD Became a Problem Far Beyond the Battlefield," *Vanity Fair*, June 2015.

Alexander Nazaryan — "Schizophrenia Doesn't Care If You're Loaded," *Newsweek*, June 26, 2014.

Patrick Quinn — "Panelists: PTSD Can't Be Cured, Only Managed," Military.com, April 24, 2013.

Emma Teitel — "Amanda Bynes and the Double Standard of Mental Illness," *Maclean's*, October 28, 2014.

Stav Ziv — "Technology's Latest Quest: Tracking Mental Health," *Newsweek*, November 12, 2014.

OPPOSING
VIEWPOINTS®
SERIES

CHAPTER 3

Is Involuntary Treatment for the Mentally Ill Ethical?

Chapter Preface

When people discuss involuntary treatment for mentally ill individuals, they usually are referring to forced hospitalization or treatment in a mental health facility. However, mentally ill people may also face other kinds of coercive restraint or treatment. In particular, mentally ill people who are experiencing an episode, or who are disruptive, may prompt family, friends, or bystanders to call the police to intervene.

It makes sense that people would move to call the police when a mentally ill person is disruptive. Unfortunately, though, in many cases, police can actually make a difficult situation worse. In August 2014, David Perry writing for CNN said that police in the previous two weeks had killed four people with mental illnesses. These deaths, Perry argues, all followed a similar pattern. A person with a mental disability was holding a weapon, police ordered the person to drop the weapon, the person did not comply, and the police shot. "Of course," Perry said, "a person struggling with his or her disability is not likely to follow verbal police commands in a moment of stress. Once the equation reached drop or die, death was inevitable." Police, Perry said, "are trained to display command presence in the face of uncertainty." They come into a situation, and they issue orders. With mentally ill people unable to obey commands, this can end in disaster.

Perry suggests that police need to be trained to deal with mental illness. They need to learn to be patient. Further, they should also, Perry suggests, use Tasers instead of guns. Tasers can be deadly as well, but they are at least less likely to do permanent harm than firearms.

Conor Friedersdorf writing in the *Atlantic* suggests that the best way to de-escalate situations with mentally ill individuals is simply not to call the police in the first place. Friedersdorf quotes a caretaker who works with mentally ill people and explains that "many police in this situation interpret non-compliance as active resistance, particularly when the individual is a young, strong man acting erratically, and their training drives them to advance on their use of force continuum." Since "some people with developmental disabilities simply don't have the cognitive skills to comply with even reasonable, lawful orders," encounters with police can escalate quickly and dangerously.

The caretaker in the article discusses a situation in which a man with a mental disability had started shouting in a supermarket; the caretaker had gotten him calmed down quickly. However, someone in the store had called the police, who came and ended up causing the situation to worsen again. The police finally Tased and arrested the man, who had already stopped creating a disturbance. Because of incidents such as this, the caretaker said, he almost always discourages staff and bystanders from ever calling the police when a mentally ill person is involved.

The following chapter examines instances of compulsory care for mentally ill individuals, including involuntary commitment and forced treatment.

> *"Homeless people with mental illnesses want treatment—forcing them instead into involuntary outpatient programs works against the very dignity and empowerment critical to recovery."*

Involuntary Treatment for the Mentally Ill Is Dangerous and Harmful

Jennifer Friedenbach

Jennifer Friedenbach is the executive director of San Francisco's Coalition on Homelessness. In the following viewpoint, she argues that a new law in California allowing for forced incarceration of the mentally ill will not help those in need. She says that San Francisco's problems with homelessness and mental illness are the result of a lack of funding and a reduction of services for the homeless and mentally ill. Forced incarceration, she says, will just use scarce resources to put individuals in a criminal justice system that will not help them. What is needed, she concludes, is not more forced incarceration, but more money for services to help the poor, homeless, and mentally ill.

As you read, consider the following questions:

1. How long does Friedenbach say Laura's Law has been in effect, and how has it been limited?

2. How does Friedenbach suggest that Laura's Law may affect black and Latino populations?

3. Why did Friedenbach title her report on homeless mentally ill people "Locked Out"?

In the past couple of years, long-term San Franciscans have often asked me why folks on the streets are in such mental distress. The answer is quite simple. Mental health and substance abuse services have been decimated in San Francisco.

Loss of Services

According to San Francisco's Health Commission, between 2007 and 2012 alone, the health department reduced behavioral health by $40 million in direct services, mostly coming out of civil service. Almost every level of services was impacted—many programs closed their doors.

A frightening reality is that the system was already stretched far beyond capacity, and services had been steadily shrinking since the late 1970s as realignment at the state level and the changing real estate market resulted in the loss of about half our board and care facilities as well as deconstruction of our then flourishing community mental health system.

The cumulative result has been staggering. The system is increasingly reliant on expensive and traumatizing stays at the locked psychiatric facility at San Francisco General Hospital and emergency room visits.

The increased acuity of people suffering from mental illnesses and addictive disorders has had a dramatic impact across the city, on emergency homeless services and neighbors alike. For the individual in crisis, however, the horror is compounded.

Laura Wilcox's Law

Scott Thorpe . . . diagnosed with schizophrenia, had killed Laura Wilcox and two others in nearby Nevada City [in 2001]. The killings attracted an unusual amount of media attention because Wilcox was an especially promising young woman, a candidate for student body president at Haverford College who had been home for the holidays and was merely filling in for a sick employee when she was killed. A bill to amend the state's commitment laws had been languishing in legislative committees for months. After [schizophrenic Mike] Bowers's truck hit the capitol building, the bill suddenly became a priority, was christened "Laura's Law" in memory of the deceased young woman, and was signed into law by Governor Gray Davis. The new law allowed, for the first time, court-ordered outpatient treatment for people with serious psychiatric disorders who refuse to take medication and are potentially dangerous. The law was aimed directly at people like . . . Scott Thorpe.

Passing legislation and implementing it, however, are two different things and sometimes only distantly related. Although Laura's Law was passed, opponents of the legislation added a provision stating that funds for existing psychiatric services could not be used to implement it. This essentially vitiated the legislation, and it consequently has been little used.

E. Fuller Torrey, The Insanity Offense:
How America's Failure to Treat the Seriously
Mentally Ill Endangers Its Citizens.
New York: W.W. Norton and Company, 2012.

The debate around the mental health system has centered around a long string of tragedies, falsely linking mental illness to violence, and focusing on forced treatment as the silver bullet that will solve the crisis. Most recently, legislation was introduced at the Board of Supervisors to enact Assembly Bill 1421, known as Laura's Law. While this law has been in effect for more than 10 years, until recently, only one small county, where Laura Wilcox lost her life, Nevada County, has implemented it. The majority of mental health providers and advocates oppose the law.

Like most Californians, advocates and mental health professionals do not believe a new bureaucratic process is the same as a new solution. AB 1421 does not address the lack of mental health treatment. It does not add funding. What it does is allow a family member, a roommate, or a police officer to petition the court, and through court order, drag someone before a judge where he or she is mandated into treatment under threat of being held in a locked facility for 72 hours. Concerns around perpetrators of domestic violence being able to use this to control their victims aside, this adds considerable costs—police, transportation, court costs and more. Resources that could go twice as far by simply expanding our treatment system.

Locked Out

However, this law goes far beyond wasting scarce resources; it traumatizes someone suffering from a health condition by putting him or her into the hands of our criminal justice system and removes fundamental rights to voice in health care decisions.

If individuals do not comply with the treatment plan, it will be up to the police to remove them from their homes. If this individual is a member of a community with a history of racial profiling and violence at the hands of the police, it can go beyond being a traumatizing experience to a potentially dangerous one. This law was implemented in New York, and studies found disturbing disparities among people of color—African Americans and Latinos were forcibly treated at much higher rates.

A year ago, I authored a study on homeless people experiencing mental illness. We surveyed hundreds of homeless people who self-identified as mentally ill, and we found that they were desperate to get help. They wanted their situations to change, and they had tried repeatedly to get treatment, to no avail. We ended up calling the report "Locked Out."

Addressing mental health issues is difficult, but not impossible. A true solution would be to build up our residential dual-diagnosis programs and radically invest in a full array of community-based mental health treatments. Programs must be nimble, as what works for some does not work for others.

A poor therapeutic relationship means little chance for success, whereas a solid relationship is grounded in trust. Homeless people with mental illnesses want treatment—forcing them instead into involuntary outpatient programs works against the very dignity and empowerment critical to recovery. AB 1421 would be disastrous for San Francisco.

> *"Why do I involuntarily commit? Because at times it is necessary."*

Involuntary Commitment Is Sometimes Necessary

John Casada

John Casada is an associate professor and psychiatrist at Abilene Christian University in Texas. In the following viewpoint, he argues that psychiatrists do not like to use involuntary hospitalization because it is coercive and damages the doctor/patient relationship. He admits, though, that in cases where a patient is in immediate danger of hurting himself or others, involuntary hospitalization may be necessary as a last resort.

As you read, consider the following questions:

1. What example does Casada give of a situation in which he would have a legal obligation to involuntarily commit a patient?

2. What are two examples Casada gives of ways in which a patient can avoid involuntary commitment?

John Casada, "Involuntary Hospitalization: One Psychiatrist's View," *The Alienist's Blog* (blog), July 6, 2011. https://thealienist.wordpress.com. © 2011 John Casada. All rights reserved. Reproduced with permission.

3. What are two examples Casada gives of ways in which patients may cause themselves to be committed?

As I have been reading other psychiatrists' blogs, I have seen heated discussions about involuntary hospitalization. Many of these posts have focused on the legal aspects of commitment or have generalized from bad experiences to "all psychiatrists." I thought I might take a little time and tell the tale from my perspective. I have also included some hints for patients wishing to avoid or obtain involuntary hospitalization.

Last Resort

There is little I dislike more than having to involuntarily hospitalize a patient. I use it literally as the last resort. I know that my chances of developing a therapeutic relationship with a patient are delayed, and perhaps prevented, by the use of power to compel hospitalization. In addition, the process involved in involuntary commitment feels overly coercive—a mode in which I am not comfortable. I do not think that I am the only psychiatrist who feels this way. I suspect that many, if not most, of my colleagues feel similarly.

If this is true, then why do I involuntarily commit? Because at times it is necessary. When I am confronted with a depressed patient who is determined to kill himself or one who is psychotic and behaving in ways that are likely to lead to imminent self-harm or harm to others, I cannot in good conscience simply let them go. This is true for both legal and moral reasons.

Legally, if I have a patient who is a threat to himself or others and this threat is due to a mental illness, I have a responsibility to act. Some have objected that psychiatrists are not all that good at predicting who is likely to act on such impulses. That is true in some cases but not in others. If I have a patient who has just tried to overdose with a lethal dose of a sufficiently toxic medication under conditions designed to avoid detection and assure death, it does not take a fortune teller to see that this patient is seriously suicidal. Certainly this is the easiest case, but it is far from uncommon. If this action occurs during the course of a mental illness, the patient deserves a chance at adequate treatment and may benefit from involuntary hospitalization. On the other hand, if their intended or ongoing behavior is not associated with a mental illness, I still may have a need to act, though this may be a legal matter (i.e., a duty to warn).

Morally, I have a duty to my patients. Those patients for whom I have had to seek involuntary hospitalization have been out of control. This does not mean out of MY control, out of their spouse's control, out of their parents' control, or out of society's control. They were out of THEIR control. They have been impulsive or based their actions on inaccurate or openly false assumptions. They have not been able to conform their behavior to reasonable requests. If they are going to make life-or-death decisions, I owe it to them to help them make sure that their decisions are based on an adequate understanding of the situation prompting their decision. And lest anyone think that this is just self-justification, I have frequently seen patients who are grateful that they were prevented from harming themselves or others and are shocked that they ever could have contemplated such actions.

Still, I hate involuntary hospitalization. It means that all other means of easing pain and making decisions have failed. Sometimes they fail because the mental health provider failed. Sometimes it failed because the patient could not comply with other alternatives. Regardless, there are no winners, only those who hopefully will not suffer as much as otherwise.

Avoiding Involuntary Hospitalization

If you have a mental illness and want to avoid involuntary hospitalization, it is pretty easy. Here are a few simple steps:

Factors for Increased Suicide Risk

> Chronic or progressive disease
> Terminal diagnosis
> Age > 65
> Mental health disorder
> Recent myocardial infarction
> Social isolation
> Lesbian, gay, bisexual, or transgender
> Stressful profession
> Substance abuse
> Past history of suicide attempt
> Family history of suicide or suicide attempt
> Creative person
> Recent assault or traumatic event
> Physical or sexual abuse
> Access to a firearm
> Self-destructive behavior
> Self-mutilation

TAKEN FROM: Roberto Canales, "Suicide Risk Assessment," Advance Healthcare Network, November 18, 2011.

---

1. Work with your mental health provider. If there is any less coercive way of assuring your safety and the safety of others, your provider will likely prefer it.

2. If your provider seems to be concerned about your safety or the safety of others around you but you do not understand why, ask your provider what he is concerned about and why. Perhaps there was a misunderstanding. Perhaps he is seeing something that signals danger but that you were not aware of.

3. Ask your provider what can be done outside of the hospital to monitor your safety and reduce risk. If your provider is comfortable that your risk of self-harm is reduced and that there are measures in place to ensure

your safety, he will be less likely to feel forced into involuntary hospitalization.

4. Ask about the appropriateness of other treatment options. Sometimes, partial hospitalization or intensive outpatient care can be helpful while retaining more freedom.

5. These steps will only work if you do them before you cause harm to yourself or others.

Achieving Involuntary Hospitalization

If you have a mental illness and WANT involuntary hospitalization, it is also pretty easy. Just follow these steps:

1. Pick a fight with the psychiatrist. Call him names. Say you have a lawyer and you'll get his license. This works just as well with psychiatrists as it does with policemen during a traffic stop.

2. Rather than show the psychiatrist that you can keep yourself and others safe, engage in a philosophical rant about how you have the right to kill yourself if you want to and that the philosophical basis for this right goes back to the Stoics.

3. Be firm in your refusal to consider why anyone should be worried about you. If you begin to show insight into how others feel about the need to protect you, the psychiatrist might lose heart and see if he can get you help outside the hospital.

4. Refuse to comply with any request by the psychiatrist. Remember, he is testing you. He wants to let you go and is looking for a good reason to believe that you can look after yourself. By not playing along or showing any self-control, you might convince him that you cannot be trusted to look out for your own interests.

> "Confining all people who have made a serious suicide attempt is particularly unjust and harmful because the vast majority of psychiatric wards do not offer effective stabilization and treatment."

Involuntary Commitment Is Unnecessary and Discriminatory

Thea Amidov

Thea Amidov is a writer for Psych Central. In the following viewpoint, she argues that involuntary commitment infringes on the civil rights of the mentally ill. Further, she says, involuntary commitment is generally ineffective; people who are suicidal are not given adequate treatment and are placed in a stressful and sometimes dangerous environment. As a result, she contends, patients often commit suicide upon release. She concludes that better treatment options, including voluntary commitment and community services, are available and should be used instead of unconstitutional imprisonment.

As you read, consider the following questions:

1. Why does Amidov object to a statistics-based approach to committing those who have made a serious suicide attempt?

2. According to the viewpoint, what did *Kansas v. Hendricks* find and mandate?

3. According to Amidov, to what kind of treatment do 70 percent of government funds go, and what does she advocate as an alternative?

Americans take considerable pride in our constitutionally guaranteed civil liberties, yet our government and institutions often abridge or ignore those rights when it comes to certain classes of people.

Deprived of Rights

According to a National Council on Disability report, people with psychiatric illnesses are routinely deprived of their civil rights in a way that no other people with disabilities are. This is particularly so in the case of people who are involuntarily committed to psychiatric wards.

Under present standards of most states, a person who is judged by a psychiatrist to be in imminent danger to self or others may be involuntarily committed to a locked psychiatric ward and detained there for a period of time. Some would argue that involuntary civil commitment is a necessary approach justified by safety and treatment concerns. Others would counter that it is an inhumane and unjustifiable curtailment of civil liberties.

Let's look at the example of recent suicide survivors in order to examine this debate in more depth.

On one side of this argument are the vast majority of mental health specialists and an uncertain percentage of former patients. They argue that forced confinement is, at times, justified by safety concerns and to ensure that proper treatment is administered. Psychiatrist E. Fuller Torrey, eminent advocate of greater use of coercive psychiatry, criticizes the reforms gained by civil rights advocates. He says that these reforms have made involuntary civil commitment and treatment too difficult and thus have increased the numbers of mentally ill people who are homeless, warehoused in jails, and doomed by self-destructive behavior to a tortured life.

DJ Jaffe claims that the high-functioning "consumertocracy" anti-psychiatry people do not speak for the severely ill and homeless. If you are suffering from serious mental illness, "freedom," Torrey and Jaffe say, is a meaningless term. Many a family member has bemoaned the difficulty in getting a loved one committed and kept safe. Torrey pleads with passion that involuntary commitment should be facilitated and the time of commitment lengthened.

No one can contest the problems that Torrey describes, but a nation dedicated to civil liberties should question the solutions he advocates. Prominent critics of coercive psychiatry include early activist psychiatrist Loren Mosher and psychologist Leighton Whitaker, the consumer organization Mindfreedom.org, consumers (or service users) such as Judi Chamberlin, and civil rights attorneys.

Damaging and Ineffective

In presenting counterarguments against the use of involuntary commitment with suicide survivors, I consider here the interlinked issues of safety and science-based medicine, as well as civil liberties and justice. Here are my concerns:

There is no reliable methodology behind the decision of whom to commit.

Despite studies and innovative tests, doctors still cannot accurately predict who will make a suicide attempt even in the near future. As Dr. Igor Galynker, associate director of [Mount Sinai] Beth Israel Department of Psychiatry said in 2011, it is amazing "how trivial the triggers may be and how helpless we are in predicting suicide." In fact, an average of one out of every two private psychiatrists loses a patient to suicide, blindsided by the action. So how do hospital psychiatrists choose which people recovering from a suicide attempt they should commit? There are patient interviews and tests, but commitment is primarily based on the statistics that a serious recent suicide attempt, particularly a violent one, predicts a 20–40 percent risk of another attempt. However, this statistics-based approach is akin to profiling. It means that those 60–80 percent who will not make another attempt will lose their liberty nonetheless. So should we accept locking up individuals when evaluation and prediction of "danger to self" is so uncertain?

Confinement does not offer effective treatment.

Erring on the side of caution and confining all people who have made a serious suicide attempt is particularly unjust and harmful because the vast majority of psychiatric wards do not offer effective stabilization and treatment. A report by the Suicide Prevention Resource Center (2011) found that there is no evidence whatsoever that psychiatric hospitalization prevents future suicides. In fact, it is widely recognized that the highest risk of a repeat attempt is soon after release from a hospital. This is not surprising, given the limited therapeutic interventions usually available on wards beyond the blanket administration of anti-anxiety and psychotropic medications. What the hospital can do is reduce the risk of suicide for the period of strict confinement. Despite this data, in *Kansas v. Hendricks* the U.S. Supreme Court found that involuntary commitment is legal even if there is an absence of treatment.

Involuntary psychiatric hospitalization is often a damaging experience.

Psychiatrist Dr. Richard Warner writes: ". . . we take our most frightened, most alienated, and most confused patients and place them in environments that increase fear, alienation, and confusion." A psychiatrist who wishes to remain anonymous told me that voluntary psychiatric programs often see patients with post-traumatic stress from their stay on a locked inpatient ward. Imagine finding yourself surviving a suicide attempt, glad to be alive, but suddenly locked up like a convicted criminal with no privacy, control over your treatment, or freedom.

Involuntary confinement undermines the patient-doctor relationship.

The prison-like environment of a locked ward and the power dynamics it entails reinforces a person's sense of helplessness, increases distrust of the treatment process, reduces medication compliance, and encourages a mutually adversarial patient-doctor relationship. Hospital psychiatrist Paul Linde, in his book, *Danger to Self*, critically labels one of his chapters, "Jailer." Yet, like some other hospital psychiatrists, he talks about the pleasure of winning cases 'against' his patients who go to mental health courts, seeking their release. The fact that judges almost always side with hospital psychiatrists undermines his victory and patient access to justice.

Finally, coercive treatment of people with mental illness is discriminatory.

Doctors do not lock up those who neglect to take their heart medications, who keep smoking even with cancer, or are addicted to alcohol. We might bemoan these situations, but we are not ready to deprive such individuals of their liberty, privacy, and bodily integrity despite their "poor" judgment. People who suffer from mental illness also are due the respect and freedoms enjoyed by other human beings.

Other Options

One might think from the widespread use of involuntary civil commitment that we have few alternatives. On the contrary, over the past decades, there have been several successful hospital diversion programs developed which use voluntary admission, peer counseling, homelike environment, and noncoercive consultative approaches, such as Soteria and Crossing Place.

Community-based cognitive therapy has been fairly effective with suicide survivors at lower cost, yet we continue to spend 70 percent of government funds on inpatient settings. Yes, many underfunded community clinics are in a disgraceful state, but the same may be said of some psychiatric hospitals.

For a nation that prides itself on its science, its innovation, and its civil rights, we have too often neglected all three in our treatment of those tormented by mental illness and despair who have tried to take their lives.

"It has been known for almost 200 years that confining mentally ill persons in prisons and jails is inhumane and fraught with problems. The fact that we have readopted this practice in the United States in recent years is incomprehensible."

Confining the Mentally Ill in Prisons Is Ineffective and Inhumane

E. Fuller Torrey et al.

E. Fuller Torrey is the executive director of the Stanley Medical Research Institute (SMRI) and founder of the Treatment Advocacy Center. In the following viewpoint, Torrey and his coauthors argue that the United States is housing huge numbers of mentally ill people in prisons. The authors say that this is detrimental for mentally ill individuals, and bad for prisons, which are not equipped to deal with the mentally ill. The authors conclude that the United States needs to reopen mental health institutions and move care of mentally ill people to these facilities.

As you read, consider the following questions:

1. According to the viewpoint, in 2012 how many inmates with mental illness were in prisons and jails, and how did this compare with patients in psychiatric hospitals?

2. What steps do public officials need to take to create a functioning mental health treatment system, according to the authors?

3. According to the viewpoint, what did a 2007 survey find about rape of mentally ill individuals in prisons?

Prisons and jails have become America's "new asylums": The number of individuals with serious mental illness in prisons and jails now exceeds the number in state psychiatric hospitals tenfold. Most of the mentally ill individuals in prisons and jails would have been treated in the state psychiatric hospitals in the years before the deinstitutionalization movement led to the closing of the hospitals, a trend that continues even today. The treatment of mentally ill individuals in prisons and jails is critical, especially since such individuals are vulnerable and often abused while incarcerated. Untreated, their psychiatric illness often gets worse, and they leave prison or jail sicker than when they entered. Individuals in prison and jails have a right to receive medical care, and this right pertains to serious mental illness just as it pertains to tuberculosis, diabetes, or hypertension. This right to treatment has been affirmed by the U.S. Supreme Court.

Numbers Are Climbing

"The Treatment of Persons with Mental Illness in Prisons and Jails" is the first national survey of such treatment practices. It focuses on the problem of treating seriously mentally ill inmates who refuse treatment, usually because they lack awareness of their own illness and do not think they are sick. What are the treatment practices for these individuals in prisons and jails in each state? What are the consequences if such individuals are not treated?

To address these questions, an extensive survey of professionals in state and county corrections systems was undertaken. Sheriffs, jail administrators, and others who were interviewed for the survey expressed compassion for inmates with mental illness and frustration with the mental health system that is failing them. There were several other points of consensus among those interviewed:

- Not only are the numbers of mentally ill in prisons and jails continuing to climb, the severity of inmates' illnesses is on the rise as well.

- Many inmates with mental illness need intensive treatment, and officials in the prisons and jails feel compelled to provide the hospital-level care that these inmates need.

- The root cause of the problem is the continuing closure of state psychiatric hospitals and the failure of mental health officials to provide appropriate aftercare for the released patients.

Among the findings of the survey are the following:

- From 1770 to 1820 in the United States, mentally ill persons were routinely confined in prisons and jails. Because this practice was regarded as inhumane and problematic, until 1970, such persons were routinely confined in hospitals. Since 1970, we have returned to the earlier practice of routinely confining such persons in prisons and jails.

- In 2012, there were estimated to be 356,268 inmates with severe mental illness in prisons and jails. There were also approximately 35,000 patients with severe mental illness in state psychiatric hospitals. Thus, the number of mentally ill persons in prisons and jails was 10 times the number remaining in state hospitals.

- In 44 of the 50 states and the District of Columbia, a prison or jail in that state holds more individuals with serious mental illness than the largest remaining state psychiatric hospital. For example, in Ohio, 10 state prisons and two county jails each hold more mentally ill inmates than does the largest remaining state hospital.

- Problems associated with incarcerating mentally ill persons include:

  - Jail/prison overcrowding resulting from mentally ill prisoners remaining behind bars longer than other prisoners

  - Behavioral issues disturbing to other prisoners and correctional staff

  - Physical attacks on correctional staff and other prisoners

  - Victimization of prisoners with mental illness in disproportionate numbers

  - Deterioration in the psychiatric condition of inmates with mental illness as they go without treatment

  - Relegation in grossly disproportionate numbers to solitary confinement, which worsens symptoms of mental illness

  - Jail/prison suicides in disproportionate numbers

  - Increased taxpayer costs

  - Disproportionate rates of recidivism

- In state prisons, treatment over objection can be accomplished administratively in 31 states through the use of a treatment review committee. Such committees were originally authorized in the case of *Washington v. Harper* upheld in 1990 by the U.S. Supreme Court. Even though this treatment mechanism is authorized in those states, it is often grossly underutilized.

- In state prisons in the other 18 states and the District of Columbia, treatment over objection requires a judicial review or transfer to a state psychiatric hospital, making such treatment much more difficult to carry out. Arkansas was the only state that refused to provide information for the survey.

- In county and city jails, the procedures for treating seriously mentally ill inmates over objection are much more varied and less clear. All counties in South Dakota and occasional counties in other states use a treatment review committee similar to that used in state prisons, and more jails could use this procedure if they wished to do so. Many jails require the inmate to be transferred to a state psychiatric hospital for treatment; since such hospitals are almost always full, such treatment does not take place in most cases.

- Prison and jail officials thus have few options. Although they are neither equipped nor trained to do so, they are required to house hundreds of thousands of seriously mentally ill inmates. In many cases, they are unable to provide them with psychiatric medications. The use of other options, such as solitary confinement or restraining devices, is sometimes necessary and may produce a worsening of symptoms. Yet, when things go wrong, as they inevitably do, the prison and jail officials are blamed. The present situation is unfair to both the inmates and the officials and is untenable.

A Mental Health System Is Needed

The ultimate solution to this problem is to maintain a functioning public mental health treatment system so that mentally ill persons do not end up in prisons and jails. To this end, public officials need to:

- Reform mental illness treatment laws and practices in the community to eliminate barriers to treatment for individuals too ill to recognize they need care, so they receive help *before* they are so disordered they commit acts that result in their arrest.

- Reform jail and prison treatment laws so inmates with mental illness can receive appropriate and necessary treatment just as inmates with medical conditions receive appropriate and necessary medical treatment.

- Implement and promote jail diversion programs such as mental health courts.

- Use court-ordered outpatient treatment (assisted outpatient treatment/AOT) to provide the support at-risk individuals need to live safely and successfully in the community.

- Encourage cost studies to compare the true cost of housing individuals with serious mental illness in prisons and jails to the cost of appropriately treating them in the community.

- Establish careful intake screening to identify medication needs, suicide danger, and other risks associated with mental illness.

- Institute mandatory release planning to provide community support and foster recovery.

- Provide appropriate mental illness treatment for inmates with serious psychiatric illness.

A model law is proposed to authorize city and county jails to administer nonemergency involuntary medication for mentally ill inmates in need of treatment.

Problems Associated with Putting Mentally Ill Persons in Prisons and Jails

The practice of putting seriously mentally ill persons into prisons and jails was abandoned in the middle of the nineteenth century in the United States. The reasons behind the abandonment of this practice included the fact that it was widely regarded as inhumane and that it also caused multiple problems for those who are mentally ill, for other prisoners, and for the prison and jail officials. In view of these well-known problems, the readoption of this practice in the late twentieth century is incomprehensible. It suggests that the learning curve among public mental health officials and elected state officials who have sanctioned this practice must be relatively flat.

Among the problems associated with placing seriously mentally ill individuals into prisons and jails are the following:

1. *Mentally ill prisoners remain in prison and jail longer than regular prisoners and thus contribute to overcrowding.*

Mentally ill prisoners remain in prison and jail longer than other prisoners because they are less likely to obtain bail and are more likely to break the rules, thus failing to get a reduction in their sentence for good behavior. In Florida's Orange County jail, the average stay for all inmates is 26 days; for mentally ill inmates, it is 51 days. In New York's Rikers Island jail, the average stay for all inmates is 42 days; for mentally ill inmates, it is 215 days. In one study, mentally ill jail inmates were twice as likely (19 percent versus 9 percent) to be charged with facility rule violations. In another study in the Washington State prisons, mentally ill inmates accounted for 41 percent of infractions, although they constituted only

19 percent of the prison population. In a county jail in Virginia, 90 percent of assaults on deputies were committed by mentally ill inmates.

2. *Mentally ill prisoners, especially those not being treated, cause major behavioral problems in prisons and jails.*

Prisons and jails are unpleasant environments even on the best of days. However, when they are overcrowded and have multiple individuals who are loudly hallucinating or manic, they become living hells. In an Oklahoma prison, it was reported that "the screams, moans and chanting are normal. The noise level rises as the sun goes down. . . . One inmate believes he is in a prisoner of war camp in Vietnam while another screams that communists are taking over the facility." A deputy at Mississippi's Hinds County Detention Center said: "They howl all night long. If you're not used to it, you end up crazy yourself." One inmate in this jail was described as having "tore up a damn padded cell that's indestructible, and he ate the cover of the damn padded cell. We took his clothes and gave him a paper suit to wear, and he ate that. When they fed him food in a Styrofoam container, he ate that. We had his stomach pumped six times, and he's been operated on twice."

Much of the behavior exhibited by mentally ill prisoners is bizarre. In Montana, a man "tried to drown himself in the jail toilet," and in California, inmates tried to escape "by smearing themselves with their own feces and flushing themselves down the toilet." Such behavior is disturbing to other prisoners and to staff, often resulting in the abuse of the mentally ill prisoner and placement in solitary confinement.

Abused and Ill

3. *Mentally ill prisoners are disproportionately abused, beaten, and/or raped.*

Mentally ill prisoners are victimized much more frequently than other prisoners. According to a 2007 prison survey, "approximately one in 12 inmates with a mental disorder reported at least one incident of sexual victimization by another inmate over a six-month period, compared with one in 33 male inmates without a mental disorder." Among female mentally ill inmates, this difference was three times higher than among male mentally ill inmates.

In 2003, Congress passed the Prison Rape Elimination Act. Subsequently, a National Prison Rape Elimination Commission undertook a five-year study of the problem. The report, issued in 2009, indicated that having a serious mental illness was a major risk factor for prison rape. It is also a major problem in jails. For example, in 2013 Joaquin Cairo, diagnosed with schizophrenia, was arrested for criminal mischief and admitted to the psychiatric unit of the Dade County jail in Miami. Within days, he suffered a fractured pelvis when he was "violently slammed into a bed by a fellow inmate during an attempted rape"; he subsequently died from the injuries.

4. *Mentally ill prisoners often become much sicker in prison and jail, especially if they are not being treated.*

As everyone who works in prisons and jails is aware, mentally ill prisoners who are not being treated often become much more symptomatic while incarcerated. Since mentally ill prisoners are permitted to refuse medication in most correctional settings except under exceptional circumstances, this causes major problems. Jail officials can thus be legally sued in many states if they forcibly medicate mentally ill prisoners without their consent, yet can also be held legally responsible for the consequences of such prisoners' psychotic behavior. It is a situation that is grossly unfair both to the mentally ill prisoners and to prison and jail officials.

One of the most dramatic illustrations of this problem is self-mutilation by mentally ill prisoners. Such incidents are not new (e.g., "Man who blinded self is moved from prison," *Atlanta Constitution*, Mar. 8, 1985), but they appear to be becoming more frequent:

Georgia, 2002: "A schizophrenic man who was jailed after wandering into traffic and knocking on doors late at night gouged out his own eyes in his cell." (*Charleston Gazette*, July 20, 2002)

North Carolina, 2007: Mario Phillips, diagnosed with schizophrenia, "cut his genitals with a razor while he was locked up waiting to go to trial." (*Fayetteville Observer*, Oct. 3, 2007)

Florida, 2007: Mark Kuzara, who "has a history of mental illness and self-mutilation," cut open his abdomen in the Polk County jail. After the wound had been stapled, "Kuzara removed the staples at the hospital with his mouth and ate them. . . . Inmates gave Kuzara pen caps, bolts and paper that he would shove into the open wound. Kuzara also made himself vomit up meals, throwing up into the open wound." (*Lakeland Ledger*, Dec. 4, 2007)

Texas, 2009: Andre Thomas, diagnosed with schizophrenia, "plucked out his right eye . . . while in the Grayson County jail five days after his arrest." Four years later, in a Texas state prison, Thomas "removed his [other] eye and ate it in a bizarre outburst." (*Wall Street Journal* blog, Mar. 20, 2008)

Minnesota, 2013: Michael Schuler, who "was psychotic and had taken methamphetamine," stabbed out both of his eyes with a pencil in the Hennepin County jail. Previously, he had been observed "standing naked in his cell, standing in his own feces, screaming gibberish," but he "refused to take his medication." (Tom Lyden, KMSP-TV bio/email, Feb. 26, 2013)

This last case illustrates the impossible situation confronting prison and jail officials on a regular basis. Mr. Schuler refused medication, so he was not involuntarily medicated, which might have led to a lawsuit brought by him. But because he was not given medication, he blinded himself and

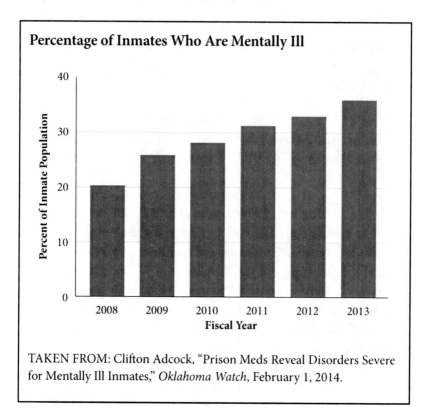

Percentage of Inmates Who Are Mentally Ill

TAKEN FROM: Clifton Adcock, "Prison Meds Reveal Disorders Severe for Mentally Ill Inmates," *Oklahoma Watch*, February 1, 2014.

then sued the jail for "providing negligent care when he was suffering from mental illness." Thus, prison and jail officials are blamed if they act and also blamed if they do not.

Solitary Confinement

5. Mentally ill prisoners are much more likely to spend time in solitary confinement.

Solitary confinement usually involves keeping prisoners in cells by themselves for 23 hours a day, allowing prisoners only one hour for showers and to exercise by themselves. Human interactions are limited, with meals usually being passed into the cell. It is variously called disciplinary segregation, administrative segregation, supermax, security housing units (SHU), special management units (SMU), control units, or simply "the hole."

As the number of seriously mentally ill prisoners has increased in recent years, an increasing number of them have ended up in solitary confinement. In New York prisons in 2003, it was estimated that approximately one-quarter of prisoners in solitary confinement were mentally ill, while in Colorado prisons in 2013 "prisoners with moderate to severe mental illness now make up the majority of those in solitary." Mentally ill prisoners who refuse to take medication are especially likely to end up in solitary confinement, both because they are so disruptive and sometimes for their own protection.

The effect of solitary confinement on mentally ill prisoners is almost always adverse. The lack of stimulation and human contact tends to make psychotic symptoms worse. Thus, it is not surprising that many of the incidents of self-mutilation and suicide by mentally ill prisoners take place when they are in solitary confinement. This has led to lawsuits against state corrections officials in several states, including Connecticut, Massachusetts, New Mexico, Ohio, Texas, and Wisconsin.

6. *Suicides in prisons and jails occur disproportionately more often among prisoners who are mentally ill.*

Suicides in prisons and jails occur, as would be expected, disproportionately among prisoners who are mentally ill. A study of 132 suicide attempters in the King County, Washington, jail system reported that 77 percent of them had a "chronic psychiatric problem," compared with 15 percent among the rest of the jail population. Interestingly, a history of substance abuse was not more prevalent among the suicide attempters compared to the rest of the jail population. Similarly, a study of 154 completed suicides in the California prison system reported that "73 percent had a history of mental health treatment."

The threat of suicide by prisoners is one of the biggest problems for corrections officials. It necessitates the careful screening of newly admitted prisoners for suicide potential and having a system of suicide watch for those at greatest risk. Since many such individuals have to be monitored every 15 minutes or watched continuously, this involves extra personnel and is one reason the cost of caring for mentally ill prisoners is much higher than the cost for other prisoners. Suicides by prisoners are also a common source of lawsuits brought against prisons and jails, thus further increasing costs.

Higher Costs

7. Mentally ill prisoners cost the county and state much more than other prisoners.

Since mentally ill prisoners stay longer than other prisoners, it is not surprising that they also cost significantly more. In Florida's Broward County jail in 2007, the difference was $130 versus $80 per day. In Texas prisons in 2003, mentally ill prisoners cost $30,000 to $50,000 per year, compared to $22,000 for other prisoners. In Washington State prisons in 2009, the most seriously mentally ill prisoners cost $101,653 each, compared to approximately $30,000 per year for other prisoners. And these costs do not include the costs of lawsuits increasingly being brought against county jails, such as the suit brought in New Jersey in 2006 by the family of a "65-year-old mentally ill stockbroker [who was] stomped to death in the Camden County jail."

Much of the cost of mentally ill prisoners comes from medication costs. In the Iowa prison system, for example, the cost of psychiatric medication increased 28-fold between 1990 and 2000. One solution to this problem is to have the family of the mentally ill prisoner supply the medication, which is allowed in some places. The risk, however, is that this could be used as a way to get illegal drugs into the prison or jail. In addition, the prison or jail could be held legally responsible and sued if something went wrong. For this reason, many jurisdictions do not allow this practice. Yet, if the mentally ill prisoner does not receive medication in a timely manner, the prison or jail may also be sued. Once again, the corrections system has been placed in the unfair position of being liable to lawsuits no matter what they do.

8. *Mentally ill prisoners are much more likely than regular prisoners to return to prison or jail in a "revolving door" phenomenon.*

Because of the widespread failure of the public mental health treatment system, most mentally ill prisoners do not receive follow-up treatment when they leave prison or jail. As a consequence, they often end up rearrested and become "frequent flyers," individuals who repeatedly recycle through the criminal justice system. Mentally ill individuals constitute at least half of all frequent flyers, according to most surveys.

A study of frequent flyers in a Florida jail defined them as having had at least "10 prior incarcerations within the prior 5 years." Among this group, "almost 50 percent were known to the jail mental health unit or mental health professionals in the community, or had been prescribed psychotropic medications at some time." Looked at another way, a study of mentally ill individuals in the Los Angeles County jail reported that 88 percent of them had had a previous psychiatric hospitalization, and 95 percent had had a previous arrest.

Mentally ill "frequent flyers" thus contribute to prison and jail overcrowding and costs. In a valiant attempt to reduce this cycle of mentally ill individuals returning to his jail, Sheriff Tom Dart, the director of the Cook County jail in Chicago, announced in 2013 that he was setting up his own mental health office and 24-hour helpline to help the mentally ill individuals who were being released from his jail.

In summary, it has been known for almost 200 years that confining mentally ill persons in prisons and jails is inhumane and fraught with problems. The fact that we have readopted this practice in the United States in recent years is incomprehensible. Prison and jail officials are being asked to assume responsibility for the nation's most seriously mentally ill individuals, despite the fact that the officials did not sign up to do this job; are not trained to do it; face severe legal restrictions in their ability to provide treatment for such individuals; and yet are held responsible when things go wrong, as they inevitably do under such circumstances. This misguided public policy has no equal in the United States.

> *"Inpatient care . . . has declined so much that it matches the service provided by prisons, institutions notorious for medical and psychological neglect."*

Mental Hospital Care Is Little Better than Prison

Chandra Bozelko

Chandra Bozelko is a poet and writer. In the following viewpoint, she argues that treatment in mental health facilities is poor and does little to rehabilitate inmates. She says that prisons are sometimes marginally better for the mentally ill, since prisons encourage inmates to work, which can be therapeutic. Bozelko concludes that moving mentally ill people from prisons to hospitals will have little beneficial effect unless the care in mental health institutions is significantly improved.

As you read, consider the following questions:

1. According to Bozelko, who was Adam Lanza?

2. What message does Bozelko say that prison work requirements send to patients?

3. What does Bozelko conclude is the problem with modern mental health care?

A s someone who was involuntarily committed for psychiatric treatment seven times in four years and served six years at York Correctional Institution in Niantic [Connecticut], I know every angle of commitment. The times I was taken to the hospital were like kidnappings; I couldn't stop to put on shoes, turn off the lights or grab a jacket.

No Treatment

The public seems convinced that the perceived link between mental illness and violence justifies essentially imprisoning someone for a medical condition. Involuntary hospitalization will become even more popular now that Connecticut's child advocate issued a report on Adam Lanza's history in November [2014]. The report revealed that treatment opportunities were missed and theorized that the shooting of 20 students and six educators at Sandy Hook Elementary School [in Newtown, Connecticut] could have been prevented if someone had intervened to force Lanza into treatment. If he went through the same experience that I did, I doubt Lanza would have warmed to psychiatric care.

Many people see Newtown as a symbol of failed mental health policy, not just for the Sandy Hook shootings but because the town saw resources shift as the Fairfield Hills Hospital for mental illness closed and Garner Correctional Institution was built in town around the same time in the mid-1990s. Deinstitutionalization just shifted patients from one type of institution to another. In fact, prisons are called the new asylums and house more mentally ill people than hospitals do.

Critics of the hyper-incarceration happening in the United States want to shift the mentally ill population back to hospitals, places where they can at least receive treatment. But, based on my experiences, there is virtually no treatment going on inside psychiatric hospitals; they provide little more than medication, the same pills delivered by prison nurses to inmates.

During my time in psychiatric hospitals, psychiatrists saw patients for about seven minutes as they did rounds with interns and residents. Patients received no individual psychotherapy. After the fleeting meeting with the doctor, patients spent the rest of the day wandering or watching TV. Social workers hired to run "groups"—group therapy sessions—were so overloaded setting up social services for discharging patients who had no support that the sessions never happened.

I received the same subpar mental health care at a prison but the atmosphere was unexpectedly more therapeutic behind bars than it was in a psych ward. Unlike hospitals, prisons require their wards to work and contribute to the correctional facility's daily upkeep. Inmates work in the kitchen preparing meals, cleaning, maintaining the grounds, shelving books in the library, unpacking commissary wares or sewing.

Prison work requirements often face criticism because the pay is so low and the jobs often unglamorous; people compare it to slavery. But work requirements send a message to prisoners: You have a responsibility, a duty to your community and you can fulfill it. You can be reliable, diligent and valuable to others even when you don't feel that way, even when everyone says you are not. I worked for almost five years loading crushed tomatoes into 200-gallon kettles because of this message.

Working in Prison

I felt useless in the hospital. Psychiatrists encourage committed hospital patients to apply for Social Security Disability, to stay out of the workforce. The social workers who should have been conducting group therapy came at me repeatedly with disability applications. I never applied but many do. In 2012, of the 10 million people receiving Social Security Disability payments, 35.5 percent or nearly 3.6 million people reportedly received it for a mental disorder. The lesson this imparts to patients is that they have little to contribute and should be sidelined—have no role in society. The message itself is stigmatizing; it tells people with mental illness that they are different, defective. Prison's work requirements make a clear impression on inmates: You are no different than anyone else and you can do it. Prison—with its innumerable faults—is a community when inmates work. Psychiatric hospitals are depositories where patients idle.

Of course, even if care in psychiatric hospitals is weak, involuntarily hospitalizing someone does incapacitate them. No one murders 26 people from a locked ward, so involuntary hospitalization might have prevented the Sandy Hook tragedy. But incapacitation is temporary and people like Adam Lanza, whose real affliction appears to have been rage, can emerge angrier because the process of being admitted is so traumatic. And if the only reason for admission is to pull someone out of society—which Lanza had done well for himself until Dec. 14, 2012—then there really is no difference between hospitals and prisons. Unless the quality of psychiatric care improves, fighting for hospital treatment over incarceration becomes a debate over geography, where these individuals should go rather than why they should be held anywhere.

This cannot mean that we should incarcerate people who have not committed crimes because prison offers the same opportunity for psychotropic medication as a hospital but more opportunities for self-edification through menial labor. Instead it highlights the fact that the inpatient care, which advocates tout and the public wants forced on certain people, has declined so much that it matches the service provided by prisons, institutions notorious for medical and psychological neglect.

The problem with modern mental health care is not that people who want it can't get it or that those who need it won't take it, but that the services they receive in the inpatient setting are inferior. Unfortunately, inpatient psychiatric care would have had little effect on Adam Lanza even if it had been forced on him.

Periodical and Internet Sources Bibliography

The following articles have been selected to supplement the diverse views presented in this chapter.

Mark Berman	"The Pennsylvania Prison System Will Stop Putting Mentally Ill Inmates in Solitary," *Washington Post*, January 8, 2015.
Meredith Cohn	"Involuntary Treatment Pursued for Mentally Ill in Maryland," *Baltimore Sun*, September 10, 2014.
Olga Khazan	"Most Prisoners Are Mentally Ill," *Atlantic*, April 7, 2015.
Renee Lewis	"US Prisons Home to 10 Times as Many Mentally Ill as in State Hospitals," Al Jazeera America, April 8, 2014.
Ronnie Polaneczky	"Mental Illness a Monumental Prison Problem," Philly.com, November 24, 2014.
Kirk Siegler	"The Divide Over Involuntary Mental Health Treatment," NPR, May 29, 2014.
Michelle Tuccitto Sullo	"Connecticut's Mentally Ill Need Services, Not Prison, Lawyers Say," *New Haven Register* (Connecticut), April 25, 2015.
Ana Swanson	"A Shocking Number of Mentally Ill Americans End Up in Prison Instead of Treatment," *Washington Post*, April 30, 2015.
Liz Szabo	"Committing a Mentally Ill Adult Is Complex," *USA Today*, January 7, 2013.
Michael Winerip and Michael Schwirtz	"For Mentally Ill Inmates at Rikers Island, a Cycle of Jail and Hospitals," *New York Times*, April 10, 2015.

OPPOSING
VIEWPOINTS®
SERIES

CHAPTER 4

What Are Issues Surrounding Violence and the Mentally Ill?

Chapter Preface

People often assume that mentally ill individuals are violent. This is thought to be the case especially when seriously mentally ill individuals experience psychotic episodes with hallucinations. Such people, it is thought, have little control over their actions and may become dangerous.

This can sometimes be true. Millet Harrison, a Texas man, murdered his mother and mutilated her body in 1994 after he heard voices telling him she was the devil. Harrison has been institutionalized for twenty years; in 2014 a judge ruled that Harrison's illness was under control with medication and that he should be released to outpatient care. The decision has caused considerable controversy, according to Michael Barajas in the *Houston Press*. Barajas reports that community members are concerned that Harrison may stop taking his medication and become a threat to himself or others. This is exacerbated by the fact that Harrison still experiences minor delusions and paranoia, though psychiatrists say he is no longer a danger.

Despite spectacular cases like Harrison's, though, research suggests that in most cases, people who experience hallucinations are not violent or dangerous. A study at the University of California, Berkeley, reviewed 305 incidents by high-risk individuals with a history of repeated violence in the United States. The researchers tried to determine how many of the violent incidents were preceded by psychosis. Even among this selected group of high-risk individuals, researchers found that only 12 percent of violent incidents were linked to psychosis or hallucinations.

"High-profile mass shootings capture public attention and increase vigilance of people with mental illness. But our findings clearly show that psychosis rarely leads directly to violence," lead author Jennifer Skeem said in a May 2015 article at the Berkeley News website. Skeem argues that risk factors for violence, such as substance abuse or childhood maltreatment, are not necessarily linked to the mentally ill but can instead be found among both those with mental illness and those without. She suggests that focusing on these risk factors, rather than on mental illness, would be a better way to reduce violence.

The authors of the viewpoints in the following chapter examine other issues related to violence and mental illness, including questions of whether insanity should be used as a defense in court and whether those diagnosed with mental illness should be denied access to firearms.

> "When an individual is determined to
> be not criminally responsible, acquittal
> via a verdict of 'not guilty by reason of
> insanity' (NGRI) is the only appropri-
> ate action."

The Insanity Defense
Is Necessary and Moral

Mental Health America

Mental Health America (MHA) is the United States' largest community-based nonprofit dedicated to mental health issues. In the following viewpoint, MHA argues that the not guilty by reason of insanity (NGRI) defense is vital. The organization says that NGRI ensures that those who are not mentally capable of understanding their actions will not be punished. Eliminating NGRI, MHA argues, is unjust. MHA adds that those who plead NGRI must be provided with adequate care and should be released as soon as they are no longer a danger. Otherwise, MHA warns, NGRI may end up being used as a punishment for crimes for which defendants have been judged not guilty.

As you read, consider the following questions:

1. What evidence does MHA use to show that the insanity defense is not overused?

2. According to the viewpoint, what is *mens rea*?

3. According to the viewpoint, what did the Supreme Court determine in *Jones v. United States*?

Society has long recognized the need to distinguish between those defendants charged with a crime who are and those who are not responsible for their acts. The insanity defense exists to identify which individuals fall into the latter category because of a mental disability. When the nature of defendants' mental impairments are such that they are not criminally responsible for their acts, it is not only unjust to impose criminal liability and punishment, but it is also ineffective. Therefore, Mental Health America's position is as follows:

- It is vital that states provide for the ongoing availability of a complete insanity defense resulting in a verdict of not guilty by reason of insanity.

- When the insanity defense does not apply, the availability of *mens rea* and diminished capacity defenses remains critically important.

- "Guilty but mentally ill" laws should be abolished as they are ineffective, unjust and misleading.

- States must provide individuals who are acquitted by reason of insanity with appropriate, recovery-based treatment, rather than treat these defendants as if they have been found guilty.

- The decision whether to plead insanity must be entirely the defendant's, although courts should take action to ensure that the defendant is capable of understanding the consequences of the decision.

The Insanity Defense

Criminal sanctions promote public safety through the deterrent effect of the punishment itself and through the stigma of a criminal conviction. Criminal sanctions also further retributivist goals. Without blameworthiness, however, punishment is not justified. When an individual is determined to be not criminally responsible, acquittal via a verdict of "not guilty by reason of insanity" (NGRI) is the only appropriate action. Since concerns about public safety and the need for treatment usually remain after acquittal, these concerns should be addressed through involuntary treatment in mental hospitals rather than through confinement in prison.

Necessary Components of a Comprehensive Insanity Defense

In order to effectively distinguish between those who are and those who are not criminally responsible for their acts, the insanity defense must contain both a "cognitive" prong and a "volitional" prong. That is, an insanity defense should exculpate both those who are unable to understand that their act is wrong, as well as those who are unable, due to mental disability, to control their actions.

Section 4.01 of the Model Penal Code (MPC), promulgated by the American Law Institute (ALI), provides a comprehensive insanity defense. Section 4.01 of the MPC remains substantially unchanged from when it was initially drafted in 1962 and currently provides as follows:

Section 4.01: Mental Disease or Defect Excluding Responsibility.

1. A person is not responsible for criminal conduct if at the time of such conduct as a result of mental disease or defect he [or she] lacks substantial capacity either to appreciate the criminality/wrongfulness of his [or her] conduct or to conform his [or her] conduct to the requirements of the law.

2. As used in this [viewpoint], the terms "mental disease or defect" do not include an abnormality manifested only by repeated criminal or otherwise antisocial conduct.

This formulation represents the consensus of American legal scholars on the appropriate scope of the insanity defense. §4.01(1) establishes both "cognitive" and "volitional" prongs, ensuring that the defense is appropriately inclusive, but §4.02(2) minimizes the risk that the defense will be over inclusive or actually encourage repeated criminal activity. Mental Health America (MHA) endorses the MPC formulation of the insanity defense.

The Insanity Defense in Practice

Despite public fears, defendants do not abuse the availability of the insanity defense. In felony cases, the defense is invoked less than 1% of the time, and even when it is employed, it is only successful 25% of the time. Further, in approximately 70% of the cases in which the defense *has* been successfully employed, the prosecution and defense have agreed on the appropriateness of the insanity plea before the trial. That individual invocations of the defense are contested relatively infrequently suggests that it is no more likely for a defendant to be incorrectly found not guilty by reason of insanity than to be incorrectly found not guilty for any other reason. Finally, there is a high likelihood of court-mandated treatment following an insanity acquittal, often lasting a substantial length of time, which serves to protect the public from defendants who may be dangerous and also to discourage people from pretending to be mentally ill in order to use the defense. These realities all refute perceptions that the insanity defense creates a loophole in criminal liability.

Although the wariness with which the public often views the insanity defense is unmerited, some states' insanity laws nonetheless reflect this suspicion. After the MPC was first promulgated, most states initially incorporated identical or substantially similar defenses into their laws. Since the late 1970s, however, many states have taken action to limit their insanity defense laws and to bring them back toward pre-MPC formulations. As of 2004, only 20 states still had insanity defense laws that incorporated the MPC formulation in its entirety or in a substantially similar fashion. As of 2010, four states (Idaho, Kansas, Montana, Utah) had eliminated the insanity defense entirely, and the remainder have limited the insanity defense to the cognitive prong.

The two-pronged protection of §4.01 is necessary in order to comply with two different constitutional requirements: due process and the prohibition against cruel and unusual punishment. In considering these issues, however, the Supreme Court has left considerable discretion to state courts. The court has indicated that states may be required to provide at least some minimal defense based on mental illness, but has not yet found a state's law to be below that minimum and has declined to specify exactly what that minimum entails. The court upheld Arizona's limited insanity defense in *Clark v. Arizona*, and denied certiorari in *Delling v. Idaho*, a case alleging that Idaho's replacement of the insanity defense with a "guilty but mentally ill" verdict constitutes a due process violation. Still, three justices dissented from the court's denial of certiorari in *Delling*, arguing that Idaho's practice does violate the Constitution. MHA agrees with this dissenting position.

MHA strongly opposes the popular, scientifically unfounded belief that mental illness predisposes a person to act violently. . . . Thus, restricting the insanity defense would not enhance public safety.

Mens Rea and Diminished Capacity Defenses

To be guilty of a crime, a person must intend to do the act that the state seeks to punish. This *"mens rea"* is a constitutional requirement, although courts have allowed states to limit it in certain ways. Thus far, the Supreme Court has held that a diminished capacity defense is not constitutionally guaranteed. But Mental Health America believes that people accused of crimes should be able to assert *mens rea* and diminished capacity defenses at trial using expert psychological evidence.

Defining the Defenses

In anything more than trivial offenses, a finding of guilt in a criminal trial generally requires some form of *mens rea*, or "guilty mind," often expressed as knowledge or intent. A defendant that does not have the required *mens rea* is not guilty of the crime. This is the *mens rea* defense.

A diminished capacity defense is different from a *mens rea* defense, but the two overlap considerably and there is not always a clear distinction between the two. A diminished capacity defense allows for mitigation of a criminal conviction based on the defendant's mental impairment, even if the insanity and *mens rea* defenses have both failed. The diminished capacity defense reflects the notion that a defendant, while guilty, may, nevertheless, be guilty of a less serious crime due to mental impairment.

The Defenses in Practice

A crime's required *mens rea* is a critical element of the offense, and without it a defendant cannot be found guilty. However, some courts have upheld state laws that interfere with this requirement. The Supreme Court in *Clark* upheld Arizona's rule that effectively precludes the use of most psychological evidence in making a *mens rea* or diminished capacity defense at trial, and instead relegated it to use only in pleading insanity. In so holding, the court simultaneously limited the defendant's ability to establish a *mens rea* defense and declared that diminished capacity defenses are not constitutionally required. As of 2007, only three states still allowed a diminished capacity defense.

As the dissent in that case noted, the practical effect of this rule is that "a person would be guilty of first-degree murder if he knowingly or intentionally . . . committed the killing under circumstances that would show knowledge or intent *but for the defendant's mental illness.*" MHA joins this dissent in arguing that such a rule is unconstitutional because it results in a guilty verdict even when the defendant did not satisfy a critical element of the crime. Moreover, even if the defendant possessed the required *mens rea*, the mental illness may remain relevant to determining the extent of his or her blameworthiness, thus necessitating a diminished capacity defense as well.

The MPC Approach

The MPC both assures a *mens rea* defense and establishes a limited diminished capacity defense in the same section, which provides as follows:

Section 4.02: Evidence of Mental Disease or Defect Admissible When Relevant to Element of the Offense; Mental Disease or Defect Impairing Capacity as Ground for Mitigation of Punishment in Capital Cases.

1. Evidence that the defendant suffered from a mental disease or defect is admissible whenever it is relevant to prove that the defendant did or did not have a state of mind that is an element of the defense.

2. Whenever the jury or the court is authorized to determine or to recommend whether or not the defendant shall be sentenced to death or imprisonment upon conviction, evidence that the capacity of the defendant to appreciate the criminality [wrongfulness] of his [or her] conduct or to conform his [or her] conduct to the requirements of law was impaired as a result of mental disease or defect is admissible in favor of a sentence of imprisonment.

Viewed in light of §4.01, §4.02 indicates that *mens rea* and diminished capacity defenses are to be available independently of the insanity defense. §4.02(2) provides a diminished capacity defense only in capital cases. While this formulation is more protective than the current law in the vast majority of states, the diminished capacity defense should not be limited to capital cases. A broader, but still sufficiently limited, defense would allow diminished capacity mitigation in all specific intent crimes, not only in capital crimes.

"Guilty but Mentally Ill" Laws

Laws establishing a "guilty but mentally ill" (GBMI) verdict are inappropriate for two reasons. First, they are inappropriate because the GBMI verdict is no different in practice from a finding of guilty. Second, they are inappropriate because this alternative to the insanity defense may confuse jurors. These fundamental problems persist whether the GBMI verdict is provided in addition to, or as a replacement for, the NGRI verdict.

A GBMI verdict provides no benefit to society or to criminal defendants because it has the same consequences as a guilty verdict. Someone found GBMI may be given any sentence that she or he could have been given if found guilty. That includes a sentence of death. Virtually every person found GBMI is sent to prison. Persons found GBMI are entitled to mental health services while imprisoned. However, they have no greater right to mental health services in prison than those simply found guilty. That is because all persons confined in prison have a constitutional right to mental health services. While GBMI statutes typically permit defendants to be transferred to mental hospitals, these provisions are permissive rather than mandatory and are rarely utilized.

Because the GBMI verdict is indistinguishable from the guilty verdict, GBMI laws serve no purpose other than to confuse jurors. Jurors may understandably believe that the GBMI

Prejudice Against the Insanity Defense

A popular public perception is that the insanity defense is easy to fake. So much of the defense depends on self-reporting of symptoms, and even expert testimony is ultimately rooted in the defendant's own words and behavior. Thus, there is widespread skepticism about excusing what would otherwise be criminal behavior, based largely on information that is provided by a defendant and that may be primarily self-serving.

Although proponents argue that the insanity defense is necessary to protect this small, despised minority who lack political power, in actuality, it is successful only approximately one-fourth of the time. Nevertheless, perceptions strongly influence reality, and it is commonly but erroneously concluded that too many defendants get off easy by using the insanity defense.

Another common attitude militating against the insanity defense involves presumptions about mental illness and dangerousness. Often, the two are conflated, based on popular prejudices about mental illness. Rather than eliciting sympathy or compassion, a defendant who claims they committed a crime because of their mental illness may end up losing their insanity claim because jurors fear him or her, and feel compelled to incarcerate in order to prevent such crimes in the future.

Frank Butler, "Insanity Defense,"
Courts, Law, and Justice. Ed. William J. Chambliss.
Thousand Oaks, CA: SAGE Publications, 2011.

verdict is a compromise between the NGRI and guilty verdicts, and thus the availability of a GBMI verdict may cause them to find a defendant GBMI when they would not have been willing to give a guilty verdict. This issue is compounded by the fact that jurors are often wary of the NGRI verdict. Although empirical evidence from actual trials is not yet available, researchers have considered, in the mock trial setting, the impact on jury preferences of the simultaneous availability of NGRI and GBMI verdicts. Research indicates that juries may use GBMI as a mechanism for "avoiding the difficult moral and social issues raised by an insanity defense."

Defendants' challenges of the GBMI verdict as a due process violation have yet to succeed. As of 2009, over 20 states provided for a GBMI verdict. Four of these states had eliminated the NGRI verdict entirely and replaced it with GBMI. The remaining 16 states with GBMI laws allow for both an NGRI verdict and a GBMI verdict. In either context, the GBMI verdict is inappropriate and seriously undermines the important policies that require maintaining the insanity and diminished capacity defenses, discussed above.

The Consequences of Pleading Insanity

An individual who is acquitted on the basis of insanity should be treated. However, it is critically important, both out of concern for promoting the public safety and out of concern for the defendant's rights, that the purpose of this treatment is rehabilitation, not to serve as a punitive alternative to imprisonment. That is, the aim of the treatment should be to eventually release an individual into the community, not to punish that individual for a crime for which the defendant has been judged not morally culpable.

In *Jones v. United States*, the Supreme Court found it constitutional for states to confine insanity acquittees in a mental health facility for periods longer than they would have been imprisoned had they been found guilty of the crime. In reality, this routinely occurs. This practice is appropriate only for as long as the additional period of confinement is clinically justified and serves a valuable rehabilitative purpose. It is critical that insanity acquittees are released when they are no longer dangerous to society.

Allowing these extended treatment periods may very well further legitimate goals, but the policy of long-term treatment after NGRI verdicts increases the risk of treatment being used as a pretext for punishment. In order to protect against this, states should adopt rigorous standards and procedures. Review boards that are as independent of the criminal justice system and of the courts as possible are one mechanism to achieve this goal. These boards serve to monitor an insanity acquittee's clinical progress and evaluate the need for continued treatment on an ongoing basis. The modern trend in states with a full insanity defense is toward use of such a system. Independent review boards serve to place the treatment and release decision-making process in the hands of those most qualified to make such determinations, and those who are most likely to act only out of public safety and treatment concerns.

The Decision to Plead Insanity

People found not guilty by reason of insanity will often be confined longer than they would have been had they been found guilty. The conditions of their confinement will also be quite restrictive. Of course, it is true that in most jurisdictions most persons with serious mental illnesses will be safer and receive better care in a mental hospital than in a prison. But respect for individual autonomy requires that the defendant be permitted to choose between these two difficult outcomes. It is critical that the decision to plead insanity is left to the defendant.

However, precisely because the decision whether to plead insanity is difficult, it is important that courts insure that criminal defendants have the capacity to make this choice and are provided with all of the relevant information. The likely length of confinement after an NGRI verdict and the likely treatment to be received are critical factors in deciding whether or not to invoke the insanity defense. And these consequences may be difficult to predict. Just as courts must ensure that defendants are competent to plead guilty and are aware of the consequences, so too should courts ensure that defendants are competent to plead insanity and are informed about the likely consequences of the plea.

Call to Action

MHA encourages policy and legal changes as necessary in order to achieve the following goals:

States should provide a full insanity defense. When defendants' mental illnesses prevent them from understanding the wrongfulness of the act or prevent them from controlling their behavior, they should be acquitted by reason of insanity. Criminal liability in these instances is neither appropriate nor effective.

Even if a defendant does not qualify for an insanity acquittal, the mental illness may remain critically relevant to the criminal proceedings. States should therefore also provide for separate, albeit related, *mens rea* and diminished capacity defenses.

"Guilty but mentally ill" verdicts are ineffective and unjust. States should neither replace the insanity defense with this disposition nor offer it as an alternative to judges and jurors considering an insanity defense.

People acquitted because of a finding of insanity should be treated in an appropriate clinical setting. The purpose of this treatment should be rehabilitative, not punitive.

Because of the weighty implications of the decision to plead insanity, the defendant must be the one to decide whether to use the insanity defense. However, courts should act to ensure that the defendant is capable of understanding the consequences of the decision. Until a defendant can do so, the state should not find him or her fit to stand trial.

> "A perpetrator should go unpunished—
> and be hospitalized instead—only if he
> is found to be completely divorced from
> reality by diagnosticians from both
> sides."

Stop the Insane Insanity Defense

Sam Vaknin

Sam Vaknin is the author of Malignant Self-Love: Narcissism Revisited *and other books on personality disorders. In the following viewpoint, he argues that the insanity defense is outdated and not congruent with modern psychiatry. He says that defendants should only be considered not guilty by reason of insanity when they are so delusional they cannot tell what is real. Otherwise, those with mental illness should be responsible for their crimes. Mental illness, he concludes, may be considered a mitigating factor during sentencing, but it should not in most cases be an excuse for crimes.*

As you read, consider the following questions:

1. According to Vaknin, who is Levi Aron, and what was his crime?

Sam Vaknin, "Stop the Insane Insanity Defense," Nydailynews.com, August 11, 2011. © 2011 New York Daily News. All rights reserved. Reproduced with permission.

2. According to the viewpoint, what three tests does the legal system apply to determine if a suspect should be held responsible for his or her actions?

3. According to Vaknin, what did the jury find in the case of Jeffrey Dahmer?

Levi Aron, who has confessed to kidnapping, murdering and dismembering 8-year-old Leiby Kletzky in Brooklyn last month [July 2011] in a crime that horrified the entire city, has one last resort: to claim that he was insane when he committed the crime.

Having just been found competent enough to eventually stand trial in Brooklyn Supreme Court, Aron and his lawyers will likely now point to a history of "psychiatric disorders," including hearing voices, in an attempt to plead NGRI ("not guilty by reason of insanity"). Yesterday, the Associated Press obtained the report of an evaluation that showed Aron to have an "apathetic" mood—as well as a schizophrenic sister, now deceased.

The insanity defense in criminal trials is nothing new. The Babylonian Talmud had this to say some 1,500 years ago: "It is an ill thing to knock against a deaf-mute, an imbecile or a minor. He that wounds them is culpable, but if they wound him they are not culpable."

But even the Talmudic rabbis would have been baffled by the modern version of the insanity defense, which has become less about compassion for the mentally ill than a loophole for criminals to escape through.

To start with, no one seems to be able to define "insanity" unequivocally. Insanity in a courtroom is not the same as the colloquial expression (i.e., "he is nuts"). To add to the confusion, it is equally distinct from the way psychiatrists use the term—which, in fact, they rarely do.

Indeed, when it comes to the antiquated insanity defense, the legal profession is completely at odds with modern psychiatry, which recognizes that "insanity" is an inaccurate term to use in describing an incredibly wide spectrum of mental states, not all of which should automatically get a criminal off the judicial hook.

The legal system applies three tests to determine whether a suspect should be held not responsible for his or her actions:

- Diminished capacity. Can the suspect tell right from wrong? Does he or she lack substantial capacity to "know and appreciate" the criminality or wrongfulness of the alleged conduct?

- Criminal intent. Did the suspect intend to act in the way that he or she did?

- Irresistible impulse. Was the suspect unable to control his or her behavior?

But many mental health scholars today regard these broad "tests" as subjective, biased and even ludicrous. What matters is whether the defendant's perception or understanding of reality is impaired. This so-called "reality test" is the only true measure of "insanity," critics say.

A perpetrator should go unpunished—and be hospitalized instead—only if he is found to be completely divorced from reality by diagnosticians from both sides, a far cry from today's insanity defense.

But the rigorous criterion of a reality test applies only to psychopaths such as Tucson shooter Jared Lee Loughner, whose reality was subverted by apparently intense bouts of psychosis (delusions, hearing voices, etc.). In these extreme instances, a criminal may be so thoroughly unaware of reality that his or her mental state really does deserve courtroom consideration.

All others should be deemed both sane and culpable for all intents and purposes, insist most psychiatrists.

Moreover, a perception and understanding of reality can coexist even with the severest forms of mental illness. Even

"My client pleads insanity, Your Honor. He must be insane, he paid me in advance."

© Marty Bucella, "My client pleads insanity, Your Honor. He must be insane, he paid me in advance," Cartoonstock.com.

when a suspect is deemed mentally ill, as long as he or she passes the reality test, that suspect should be held criminally responsible.

The serial killer Jeffrey Dahmer, accused of killing 17 young men and boys, pleaded NGRI in 1992. Despite obvious mental health troubles, however, the jury rightly found that he was responsible for his actions and sentenced him to more than 900 years in prison.

Consider, also, the cases of the Norway shooter Anders Behring Breivik or Unabomber Ted Kaczynski. Both have coherent worldviews, a consistent internal logic and highly complex ethical codes. Their philosophy may be repellent or outlandish, but that alone does not make them insane.

Breivik, for instance, is not delusional. Yet his lawyer is seriously considering using the insanity defense.

This is not to say that a defendant's mental state at the time of the crime is irrelevant: He or she may have held mistaken (even delusional) beliefs or may have misread the situation, may have been misinformed, may have been under the influence of mind-altering drugs, may have lacked criminal intent, may have been unable to tell right from wrong or to control his or her urges.

A troubled mental state can be accounted for during the sentencing, but the all-purpose insanity defense is an outdated tactic that poorly serves justice and science alike.

> *"For people with severe psychiatric illness, taking an antipsychotic medication appears to drive down the risk of engaging in criminal violence."*

Better Mental Health Care Can Reduce Violence

Melissa Healy

Melissa Healy is a health and science reporter for the Los Angeles Times. *In the following viewpoint, she reports on a study that shows links between violence and mentally ill patients who are not taking medication. Healy argues that mentally ill people are not as prone to violence as the media often suggest. However, mentally ill people are also not as nonviolent as advocates sometimes claim. In particular, patients with serious mental disorders and substance abuse problems may be violent. The study also shows that patients who are not treating serious mental illnesses may be more likely to commit acts of violence.*

As you read, consider the following questions:

1. According to Healy, how much greater is the chance that people with schizophrenia will commit violent acts compared to the general population?

2. What records did the researchers use to perform the study discussed by Healy?

3. What could cause the drop in crime in mentally ill individuals other than medication, according to the researchers?

For people with severe psychiatric illness, taking an antipsychotic medication appears to drive down the risk of engaging in criminal violence, a large study has found. And for patients diagnosed with bipolar disorder, a mood-stabilizing medication has the same effect.

Link Between Violence and Mental Illness

Those findings, emerging from a large and comprehensive study conducted in Sweden, suggest that when used by those with serious mental illness, these widely prescribed medications not only tame delusions, help restore emotional order and prevent relapses—they may also reduce the risk to the communities in which these patients live.

The study was published Wednesday [in May 2014] in the medical journal the *Lancet*.

The truth about mental illness and violence lies somewhere between two extremes. In the wake of a mass shooting and the inevitable media focus on a perpetrator's mental health, it would be easy to assume that psychiatric illness is the principal cause of community violence. But that is not the case, researchers say.

On such occasions, mental health advocates—fearing an uptick in stigma against those with mental illness—say that those with psychiatric illness are more likely to be victims

How Much Various Factors Are to Blame for Mass Shootings in the United States

Thinking about mass shootings that have occurred in the United States in recent years, from what you know or have read, how much do you think each of the following factors is to blame for the shootings—a great deal, a fair amount, not much, or not at all?

Percent a Great Deal to Blame	Jan. 14–16, 2011 %	Sept. 17–18, 2013 %	Change pct. pts.
Failure of the mental health system to identify individuals who are a danger to others	48	48	0
Easy access to guns	46	40	–6
Drug use	42	37	–5
Violence in movies, video games, music lyrics	31	32	+1
Spread of extremist viewpoints on the Internet	32	29	–3
Insufficient security at public buildings including businesses and schools	n/a	29	n/a
Inflammatory language from prominent political commentators	19	18	–1

TAKEN FROM: Lydia Saad, "Americans Fault Mental Health System Most for Gun Violence," Gallup, September 20, 2013.

than perpetrators of violence, leaving an impression that is not entirely accurate. For patients with schizophrenia and other related psychoses, a recent study estimated that the risk of perpetrating violence against other people is fourfold that of the general population. That added risk appears to be concentrated mainly among those with major mental illness who also suffer from alcohol and substance abuse disorders.

Against that backdrop, little research has been conducted on how psychiatric medication affects the heightened risk of aggression or violence in some with mental illness, and whether some medications might do a better job at driving down that risk. Clinical trials that randomly assign people with diagnosed mental illness to treatment and non-treatment arms wouldn't be ethical. And there's a flaw in studies that merely compare the rate of violent crime perpetrated by medicated psychiatric patients with that of similar patients taking none: Other key differences in these two populations—say, economic status or social support—might account for the two groups' different propensities to commit crime.

On Medication vs. Off

So in this study, Oxford University psychiatrist Dr. Seena Fazel and his Swedish collaborators decided to use Sweden's comprehensive records of health care, pharmaceutical dispensing and criminal cases to compare the arrest and conviction records of patients with schizophrenia, bipolar disorder and related psychoses when they were on medications with their arrest and conviction records while off medication. They also did a population-wide comparison of medicated patients' violent criminal behavior rates with those of unmedicated patients.

Among the study's 82,647 subjects—all of them prescribed an antipsychotic or mood-stabilizing drug at some point between 2006 and 2009—routinely taking an antipsychotic drug was linked to a 29% reduced probability of being convicted of a drug-related charge, a 22% decline in convictions for any crime, and a 26% reduction in the likelihood of arrest on suspicion of having committed a violent crime. Subjects seeing these reductions took such new generation antipsychotics as quetiapine (marketed at Seroquel), olanzapine (Zyprexa), risperidone (Risperdal) and aripiprazole (Abilify), or older antipsychotics such as haloperidol (Haldol) or chlorpromazine (Thorazine).

Mood-stabilizing drugs—medications ranging from lithium to neuroleptics such as valproic acid (Depakote), lamotrigine (Lamictal), carbamazepine (Tegretol) and oxcarbazepine (Trileptal)—were on average less powerfully linked to lower crime rates. Compared with periods during which they were unmedicated, when subjects were taking mood-stabilizing drugs, they were, on average, 32% less likely to be convicted of a drug-related crime, 17% less likely to be committed of any crime and 13% less likely to be arrested on suspicion of a violent crime.

When subjects taking one of these mood-stabilizing drugs also had a diagnosis of bipolar disorder, however, the reduction in arrests and convictions was far more robust, researchers said.

The study's authors acknowledge that their study design does not establish medication as the clear cause of a patient's lower propensity to crime. Other factors—including the more regular interaction with a psychiatrist that comes with medication—might help explain the effect.

But the fact that violence was reduced across such a range of patients taking so many different kinds of drugs suggests that in addition to providing relief of psychotic symptoms, these drugs may help tamp down "behavioral traits of anger and hostility" in many patients who take them, the authors said.

"*The new rules and proposals perpetuate the assumption that people with mental illness are dangerous; instead of making people safer, the requirements may hurt efforts to get the mentally ill treatment.*"

Guns—Not the Mentally Ill—Kill People

Abby Rapoport

Abby Rapoport is a journalist and former staff writer for the American Prospect. In the following viewpoint, she argues that mentally ill people are not more likely than others to commit gun violence. Targeting mentally ill individuals, she says, can be dangerous because it distracts from the broader problem of gun availability. Also, many laws regulating guns target mentally ill people who are committed to facilities or who are receiving treatment; these laws are counterproductive, Rapoport argues, since mentally ill people receiving treatment are substantially less likely to commit violence.

As you read, consider the following questions:

1. According to Rapoport, who are Wayne LaPierre and Ann Coulter, and what did they say about the connection between gun violence and mental illness?

2. What states does Rapoport mention as considering restrictive legislation on the mentally ill?

3. What is one positive aspect of the national conversation about mental illness, according to Rapoport?

After a year of violent tragedies that culminated with the elementary school shooting in Newtown, Connecticut [in December 2012], America is finally having a conversation about gun control. For the many who want to decrease access to firearms in the wake of several mass shootings, new laws being proposed around the country to limit and regulate guns and ammunition represent a momentous first step.

But running through the gun control debate is a more delicate conversation: how to handle mental health treatment in America. Among both Democrats and Republicans, in both the pro-gun and anti-gun lobbies, there's a widespread belief that mental health treatment and monitoring is key to decreasing gun violence. Shining more light on the needs and struggles of the mentally ill would normally be a positive change; mental health programs and services have been cut year after year in the name of austerity. But in the context of gun violence, those with mental illness have become easy scapegoats. Rather than offering solutions to the existing problems that patients and providers face, policy makers instead promise to keep guns out of the hands of the mentally ill. The trouble is, that often means presenting policies that are actually detrimental to mental health treatment—threatening doctor-patient confidentiality, expanding forced treatment rather than successful voluntary programs, and further stigmatizing people with databases that track who's been committed to hospitals or mental institutions.

The National Rifle Association [of America, NRA] has led the charge to blame those with mental illness. "The truth is that our society is populated by an unknown number of genuine monsters—people so deranged, so evil, so possessed by voices and driven by demons that no sane person can possibly ever comprehend them," NRA executive vice president Wayne LaPierre said at his December 21 [2012] press conference. "How can we possibly even guess how many, given our nation's refusal to create an active national database of the mentally ill?" [Social and political commentator] Ann Coulter was more succinct: "Guns don't kill people—the mentally ill do."

It's not just the NRA and the right wing who are turning mentally ill Americans into political pawns. See, for instance, New York's new gun control law, the first passed after Newtown. In addition to banning assault weapons and semiautomatic guns with military-level components, the legislation requires therapists, nurses and other mental health care providers to alert state health authorities if they deem a patient is a danger to self or others. That would then allow the state to confiscate the person's guns. The measure broadens the confiscation powers to include those who voluntarily seek commitment to a mental health facility—in other words, the people who get help without being forced. Finally, it strengthens Kendra's Law, which allows the courts to involuntarily commit the mentally ill.

Other states will very likely follow suit. Legislatures in Ohio and Colorado will both consider measures to make it easier to commit people. Maryland governor Martin O'Malley wants to broaden the range of people banned from owning guns to include those who have been civilly committed to mental institutions at any time. Policy makers in Louisiana, Massachusetts, Pennsylvania, Rhode Island, and Utah have also proposed measures aimed specifically at keeping the mentally ill from getting guns.

The new rules and proposals perpetuate the assumption that people with mental illness are dangerous; instead of making people safer, the requirements may hurt efforts to get the mentally ill treatment. For instance, the expanded reporting requirements mean mental health providers must alert officials if a patient may harm herself or others. Law enforcement officials can then show up and confiscate any guns the patient owns. Mental health providers are already supposed to report if a patient seems in imminent danger of doing harm, but the new law broadens that rule. It could easily chip away trust between therapists and their patients. The threat of gun confiscation may make it less likely that folks like policemen and veterans suffering from trauma get help, since many are gun owners. "It's very hard to get people to come forward and get help," says Ron Honberg, the national director for policy and legal affairs at the mental health advocacy group National Alliance on Mental Illness. "If they're aware that by seeking help they're going to lose their right to have a gun, we're concerned it's going to have a chilling effect."

It's also not likely to slow down the violence. Predicting murderous behavior is extremely difficult and most of the time, the providers can't do it accurately. "We're making an assumption that violence can be predicted," Honberg says. In fact, it's *lack* of treatment, combined with substance abuse and a history of violence, that tend to be the best predictors of future violence. Yet many of New York's new laws—like the reporting requirements and the push to put more mentally ill people in government databases—target those who are already getting help.

The issue is not that mental health advocates want to arm more people but that those with mental illness are being singled out by often well-intended gun control measures, which could increase the stigma around getting help. By fo-

The Failure of Gun Control

The gun control campaign has always had many assets that are important to movement building, including sympathetic elected officials willing to champion the cause, shootings and crime waves that dramatized the problem, majority support among the public for tighter firearms restrictions, and single- and multi-issue organizations capable of mobilizing the masses. But these critical movement ingredients—opportunities, organizations, and opinion—were not enough. Unlike other movements, such as those against tobacco, smoking, and abortion, the gun control campaign struggled to obtain patronage, to craft a resonant issue frame, and to settle on a strategy that could deliver movement-building victories. As a result, even as Americans were bombarded every day by reports of violence, and even as one-third of Americans reported that someone close to them had been shot, gun control remained remote—difficult to relate to, difficult to rally around. Somewhat counterintuitively, gun control did not inspire a true social movement, in part because its elite leaders for decades did not think one necessary and in part because their opponents, rightly sensing what a gun control movement could accomplish if it did coalesce, used their political advantages to keep that movement from arising.

Kristin A. Goss, Disarmed:
The Missing Movement for Gun Control in America.
Princeton, NJ: Princeton University Press, 2006.

cusing on keeping guns out of the hands of the mentally ill specifically—and not those who have histories of substance abuse, domestic violence, and other predictors of violent behavior—these laws perpetuate the idea that the mentally ill are an overwhelming threat. So does a recent report from Mayors Against Illegal Guns, which highlights the gaps in reporting mentally ill people to the NICS [National Instant Criminal Background Check System] database; in red pullout text, it prominently displays examples of mentally ill people responsible for violence.

The stereotype that the mentally ill are very violent is simply incorrect. According to the National Institute of Mental Health, people with severe mental illness, like schizophrenia, are up to three times more likely to be violent, but "most people with [severe mental illness] are not violent and most violent acts are not committed by people with [severe mental illness.]" On the whole, those with mental illness are responsible for only 5 percent of violent crimes.

"People with mental illness are so much more likely to be victims of crimes than perpetrators that it's almost immeasurable," says Debbie Plotnick, the senior director of state policy at Mental Health America, an advocacy group for mental health treatment. According to one study, people with mental illness are 11 times more likely to be the victims of violence.

Fortunately, the national conversation hasn't been entirely negative. Advocates see an undeniable opportunity to get more funding and attention to mental health services. For the first time in recent memory, governors and lawmakers across the political spectrum are pushing for more dollars to help those with mental illness.

That's particularly important because over the past four years, $4.35 billion was cut in funding for Medicaid mental health funding, substance abuse, housing, and other mental health programs at the state and federal level. Now, even Kansas's ultraconservative governor Sam Brownback is pushing for $10 million more for mental health care. South Carolina governor Nikki Haley, a Tea Party favorite, has also argued for an increase in funding. In Oklahoma, Colorado,

Minnesota, and Missouri, legislatures will very likely consider investing more heavily in treatment of mental illness.

The investment is badly needed. Over the years, most states have cut back to only providing emergency and crisis care for mental illnesses. That's both expensive and ineffective. Harvey Rosenthal, executive director of the New York Association of Psychiatric Rehabilitation Services, says the most successful programs are those that focus on getting a patient help wherever they are, while providing other necessities like housing. For instance, the "housing first" model provides housing to people who might not otherwise qualify and then layers on services like mental health and substance abuse treatment. Such programs, like New York's Pathways to Housing, have an astounding 85 percent retention rate, and according to Rosenthal, they're successful because they tailor to a person's specific needs rather than telling patients, "You're mentally ill and you need medicine."

More attention to the cracks in care for the mentally ill is a good thing. While it may not have much to do with gun violence, there *is* a serious mental health care problem in the country.

Periodical and Internet Sources Bibliography

The following articles have been selected to supplement the diverse views presented in this chapter.

Keith Ablow	"Our Mental Health Care System Is a Joke—Even Mass Murderer Elliot Rodger Slipped Through the Cracks," Fox News, May 27, 2014.
Lois Beckett	"What We Actually Know About the Connections Between Mental Illness, Mass Shootings, and Gun Violence," *Pacific Standard*, June 10, 2014.
Danny Cevallos	"Don't Rely on Insanity Defense," CNN, February 12, 2015.
Maria Konnikova	"Is There a Link Between Mental Health and Gun Violence?," *New Yorker*, November 19, 2014.
Morgan Lowe	"Is Insanity Plea Just Manipulation?," *Denver Post*, March 25, 2015.
Jeremy Meyer	"Do Insanity Pleas Let Killers Out Too Early?," *Denver Post*, April 11, 2015.
Mel Robbins	"The Real Gun Problem Is Mental Health, not the NRA," CNN, June 25, 2014.
Frank S. Robinson	"Not Buying the Insanity Plea," *Humanist*, November–December 2014.
Margot Sanger-Katz	"Why Improving Mental Health Would Do Little to End Gun Violence," *National Journal*, January 26, 2013.
Douglas Starr	"Can You Fake Mental Illness?," *Slate*, August 7, 2012.
Rebecca Terrell	"Playing Mind Games with the Second Amendment," *New American*, July 17, 2014.

For Further Discussion

Chapter 1

1. In his viewpoint, Victor Carrion says that 30 percent of children in violent communities have symptoms of post-traumatic stress disorder, which can include learning and behavior problems. Carrion says that a physician who is unaware of the fact that a child experienced trauma, and noting the child's cognitive and learning difficulties, may diagnose attention-deficit/hyperactivity disorder (ADHD) instead of PTSD. How does a diagnosis of ADHD instead of PTSD present problems for the patient? Explain.

2. Bruce Levine argues that there has been a huge increase in mental illness diagnoses in recent years, saying that doctors are overdiagnosing normal sadness and distress as mental illness. Do you agree with Levine's argument? Why, or why not?

Chapter 2

1. Margarita Tartakovsky said that 74 percent of patients with schizophrenia who were prescribed pharmaceuticals stopped taking their medication within the first eighteen months of treatment. What are some of the reasons patients stop taking their medication? What do you think doctors can do to encourage their patients to take the prescribed medication?

2. What does Rachel Pruchno mean when she says in her viewpoint that cognitive behavioral therapy (CBT) may be a "placebo effect"? Explain. Do you think CBT can be an effective treatment for managing mental illness? Why, or why not?

3. Owen Jones says that men in the poorest socioeconomic conditions are ten times more likely to kill themselves

than men in affluent circumstances. Why do you think men are more likely to kill themselves if they are poor? Explain your reasoning.

Chapter 3

1. Thea Amidov presents several arguments against involuntary commitment. Choose two of Amidov's arguments and offer a rebuttal to each. Support your arguments with text from other viewpoints in the chapter.

2. In her viewpoint, Chandra Bozelko compares her experiences in both mental hospitals and prison. She says that the atmosphere in prison was more therapeutic than in the hospital's psychiatric ward. What evidence does Bozelko offer to support this claim? Does Bozelko think that involuntary commitment is beneficial? Explain.

Chapter 4

1. Mental Health America (MHA) argues that the "guilty but mentally ill" (GBMI) verdict is inappropriate for two reasons. What are those two reasons? Do you agree with MHA that GBMI verdicts are ineffective and unjust? Explain why, or why not.

2. In his viewpoint, Sam Vaknin argues that the "tests"—diminished capacity, criminal intent, and irresistible impulse—are subjective and biased and should not be used to determine whether a suspect should be held responsible for his actions. Vaknin says what matters is whether the defendant's perception or understanding of reality is impaired. Do you agree with Vaknin's argument? Why, or why not?

3. After reading the viewpoint by Abby Rapoport, do you think that mentally ill individuals should be allowed to purchase guns? Explain your reasoning, citing text from the viewpoint to support your answer.

Organizations to Contact

The editors have compiled the following list of organizations concerned with the issues debated in this book. The descriptions are derived from materials provided by the organizations. All have publications or information available for interested readers. The list was compiled on the date of publication of the present volume; the information provided here may change. Be aware that many organizations take several weeks or longer to respond to inquiries, so allow as much time as possible.

American Academy of Child and Adolescent Psychiatry (AACAP)
3615 Wisconsin Avenue NW, Washington, DC   20016-3007
(202) 966-7300 • fax: (202) 966-2891
website: www.aacap.org

The nonprofit American Academy of Child and Adolescent Psychiatry (AACAP) is a professional medical association dedicated to promoting mentally healthy children, adolescents, and families. Since its inception in 1953, the AACAP has worked to treat millions of American youth suffering from mental, behavioral, and developmental disorders. The AACAP works through advocacy, education, and research to promote the mentally healthy development of America's youth. It publishes the monthly *Journal of the American Academy of Child and Adolescent Psychiatry*. The Families and Youth section of the AACAP website provides resources such as videos, fact sheets, position papers, and abstracts from professional journals on topics such as anxiety disorders, bipolar disorder, depression, and substance abuse.

American Psychiatric Association (APA)
1000 Wilson Boulevard, Suite 1825, Arlington, VA   22209
(703) 907-7300
e-mail: apa@psych.org
website: www.psychiatry.org

Founded in 1844, the American Psychiatric Association (APA) is the world's largest psychiatric organization. With more than thirty-six thousand psychiatrists who are dedicated to studying the nature, treatment, and prevention of mental disorders, the APA helps create mental health policies, distributes information about psychiatry, and promotes psychiatric research and education. It publishes the monthly *American Journal of Psychiatry* and the bimonthly *Psychiatric News*. Its website features the *Healthy Minds, Healthy Lives* blog with articles such as "Mental Illness by the Numbers" and "How Psychotherapy Changes the Brain."

American Psychological Association (APA)

750 First Street NE, Washington, DC   20002-4242
800-374-2721
website: www.apa.org

With more than 120,000 members, the American Psychological Association (APA) is the largest scientific and professional organization representing psychology in the United States. Its mission is to advance the creation, communication, and application of psychological knowledge to benefit society and improve people's lives. The APA produces more than seventy journals, including its flagship publication *American Psychologist*. In addition, its website offers research on topics such as stress, post-traumatic stress disorder, schizophrenia, bipolar disorder, suicide, and violence.

Carter Center

One Copenhill, 453 Freedom Parkway, Atlanta, GA   30307
(404) 420-5100
e-mail: carterweb@emory.edu
website: www.cartercenter.org

The Carter Center was founded in 1982 by former president Jimmy Carter and his wife, Rosalyn. The center works to promote awareness of mental illnesses and to reduce the stigma and discrimination against individuals who have mental disorders. It works to promote awareness about mental health issues, inform public policy, and achieve equity for mental health care comparable to other health care. The center sponsors the Rosalynn Carter Fellowships for Mental Health Journalism to encourage reporting on topics related to mental health. In addition, *The Carter Center Blog*, featured on the center's website, offers articles such as "Progress, Trends, and Challenges in Mental Health," "Living with Schizophrenia," and "Fighting Stigma Against People with Mental Illness."

Mental Health America

2000 N. Beauregard Street, 6th Floor, Alexandria, VA   22311
(703) 684-7722 • fax: (703) 684-5968
e-mail: infoctr@mentalhealthamerica.net
website: www.mentalhealthamerica.net

Mental Health America (MHA), formerly known as the National Mental Health Association, is the country's leading nonprofit dedicated to helping Americans live mentally healthier lives through advocacy, public education, and service. With more than 220 affiliates across the United States, MHA promotes prevention for all; early identification and intervention for those at risk; integrated health and behavioral health care for those who need it; and recovery as a goal. The MHA website provides news, press releases, and position statements. It features the MHA blog *Chiming In*, which offers articles such as "What Did We Learn from Sandy Hook?," "New Thinking on Mental Illness Diagnoses," and "Bring Back the Asylum?"

National Alliance on Mental Illness (NAMI)

3803 N. Fairfax Drive, Suite 100, Arlington, VA   22203
(703) 524-7600 • fax: (703) 524-9094
website: www.nami.org

Founded in 1979, the National Alliance on Mental Illness (NAMI) is the nation's largest grassroots mental health organization dedicated to improving the lives of the millions of Americans affected by mental illness. With more than one thousand chapters across the United States, NAMI adheres to the position that severe mental illnesses are biological brain diseases and that mentally ill people should not be blamed or stigmatized for their conditions. The alliance produces the magazine *NAMI Advocate*, which is published three times a year for members, as well as numerous online newsletters. The NAMI website offers a Fact Sheet Library with online access to information on mental health topics.

National Institute of Mental Health (NIMH)

Science Writing, Press, and Dissemination Branch
6001 Executive Boulevard, Room 6200, MSC 9663
Bethesda, MD   20892-9663
866-615-6464 • fax: (301) 443-4279
e-mail: nimhinfo@nih.gov
website: www.nimh.nih.gov

The National Institute of Mental Health (NIMH) is part of the National Institutes of Health (NIH), a component of the US Department of Health and Human Services. NIMH's mission is to transform the understanding and treatment of mental illnesses through basic and clinical research, paving the way for prevention, recovery, and cure. Its website contains news, statistics, and information about its research, as well as the *Director's Blog*, which features the articles "Can We Prevent Psychosis?," "Getting Serious About Mental Illness," and "Healing Invisible Wounds: An Action Plan."

Substance Abuse and Mental Health Services Administration (SAMHSA)

1 Choke Cherry Road, Rockville, MD   20857
877-726-4727
website: www.samhsa.gov

The Substance Abuse and Mental Health Services Administration (SAMHSA) is the agency within the US Department of Health and Human Services whose mission is to reduce the impact of substance abuse and mental illness on America's communities. SAMHSA was established by Congress in 1992 to make substance use and mental disorder information, ser-

vices, and research more accessible. The SAMHSA website offers articles from its national newsletter *SAMHSA News*, which
features articles such as "Improving Mental Health in America"
and "Preventing Suicide: Following Up After the Crisis." The
website also provides a link to MentalHealth.gov, which provides one-stop access to US government mental health information as well as government-issued news releases, editorials,
speeches, and fact sheets.

Treatment Advocacy Center
200 N. Glebe Road, Suite 801, Arlington, VA   22203
(703) 294-6001 • fax: (703) 294-6010
e-mail: info@treatmentadvocacycenter.org
website: www.treatmentadvocacycenter.org

The Treatment Advocacy Center is a national nonprofit organization dedicated to eliminating barriers to the timely and
effective treatment of severe mental illnesses. It promotes laws,
policies, and practices for the delivery of psychiatric care and
supports the development of innovative treatments for and
research into the causes of severe and persistent psychiatric illnesses. The center's website offers reports, studies, and back-
grounders, including "More Mentally Ill Persons Are in Jails
and Prisons than Hospitals" and "Are Mass Killings Associated
with Untreated Mental Illness Increasing?"

World Health Organization (WHO)
525 Twenty-Third Street NW, Washington, DC   20037
(202) 974-3000 • fax: (202) 974-3663
e-mail: info@who.int
website: www.who.int

The World Health Organization (WHO) is an agency of the
United Nations formed in 1948 with the goal of creating and
ensuring a world where all people can live with high levels of
both mental and physical health. WHO's Mental Health Gap
Action Programme (mhGAP) seeks to improve services for
mental, neurological, and substance use disorders for countries that have especially low incomes. The program asserts

that with proper care, psychosocial assistance, and medication tens of millions of people could be treated for mental illness, even where resources are scarce. Mental health publications such as "Building Back Better: Sustainable Mental Health Care After Emergencies" can be downloaded for free from the WHO website. Its website also includes numerous reports and discussions of mental health issues throughout the world.

Bibliography of Books

Joie D. Acosta et al.
Mental Health Stigma in the Military. Santa Monica, CA: RAND Corporation, 2014.

Aaron T. Beck, Neil A. Rector, Neal Stolar, and Paul Grant
Schizophrenia: Cognitive Theory, Research, and Therapy. New York: Guilford Press, 2011.

Joan Busfield
Mental Illness. Malden, MA: Polity Press, 2011.

Daniel Carlat
Unhinged: The Trouble with Psychiatry—A Doctor's Revelations About a Profession in Crisis. New York: Free Press, 2010.

Dennis Charney, Pamela Sklar, Joseph Buxbaum, and Eric Nestler, eds.
Neurobiology of Mental Illness. 4th ed. New York: Oxford University Press, 2014.

Victoria Costello
A Lethal Inheritance: A Mother Uncovers the Science Behind Three Generations of Mental Illness. New York: Prometheus Books, 2012.

Jacqueline Maria Ellison
Mental Illness. Bloomington, IN: AuthorHouse, 2015.

Erin P. Finley
Fields of Combat: Understanding PTSD Among Veterans of Iraq and Afghanistan. Ithaca, NY: Cornell University Press, 2011.

Allen Frances — *Saving Normal: An Insider's Revolt Against Out-of-Control Psychiatric Diagnosis, DSM-5, Big Pharma, and the Medicalization of Ordinary Life.* New York: HarperCollins, 2013.

Milt Greek — *Schizophrenia: A Blueprint for Recovery.* Seattle, WA: CreateSpace, 2012.

Michael T. Keene — *Mad House: The Hidden History of Insane Asylums in 19th-Century New York.* Fredericksburg, VA: Willow Manor Publishing, 2013.

Bessel van der Kolk — *The Body Keeps the Score: Brain, Mind, and Body in the Healing of Trauma.* New York: Viking, 2014.

Jutta Lindert and Itzhak Levav, eds. — *Violence and Mental Health: Its Manifold Faces.* New York: Springer, 2015.

Richard J. McNally — *What Is Mental Illness?* Cambridge, MA: Harvard University Press, 2011.

Neela Redford — *Challenged by Mental Illness: Resting in God's Love.* Mustang, OK: Tate Publishing, 2014.

Andrew Scull — *Madness in Civilization: A Cultural History of Insanity, from the Bible to Freud, from the Madhouse to Modern Medicine.* Princeton, NJ: Princeton University Press, 2015.

Susan Sheehan — *Is There No Place on Earth for Me?* 2nd ed. New York: Vintage, 2014.

Nancy Sherman — *Afterwar: Healing the Moral Wounds of Our Soldiers.* New York: Oxford University Press, 2015.

Thomas S. Szasz — *The Myth of Mental Illness: Foundations of a Theory of Personal Conduct.* New York: Harper Perennial, 2010.

E. Fuller Torrey — *American Psychosis: How the Federal Government Destroyed the Mental Illness Treatment System.* New York: Oxford University Press, 2014.

E. Fuller Torrey — *The Insanity Offense: How America's Failure to Treat the Seriously Mentally Ill Endangers Its Citizens.* New York: W.W. Norton, 2012.

Pete Walker — *Complex PTSD: From Surviving to Thriving.* Seattle, WA: CreateSpace, 2013.

Ethan Watters — *Crazy Like Us: The Globalization of the American Psyche.* New York: Free Press, 2010.

Robert Whitaker — *Anatomy of an Epidemic: Magic Bullets, Psychiatric Drugs, and the Astonishing Rise of Mental Illness in America.* New York: Crown Publishing Group, 2010.

Robert Whitaker — *Mad in America: Bad Science, Bad Medicine, and the Enduring Mistreatment of the Mentally Ill.* 2nd ed. New York: Basic Books, 2010.

| Anthony Wilkenson | *Schizophrenia: Understanding Symptoms Diagnosis & Treatment.* Seattle, WA: CreateSpace, 2014. |
| Paris Williams | *Rethinking Madness: Towards a Paradigm Shift in Our Understanding and Treatment of Psychosis.* San Rafael, CA: Sky's Edge, 2012. |

Index

M

N

O

CPSIA information can be obtained
at www.ICGtesting.com
Printed in the USA
FFOW05n0630060116

9 780737 775136